LIBERAL CHRISTIANITY
AT THE CROSSROADS

Books by John B. Cobb, Jr.
Published by The Westminster Press

Liberal Christianity at the Crossroads

*The Theology of Altizer:
  Critique and Response* (Ed.)

God and the World

The Structure of Christian Existence

*A Christian Natural Theology:
  Based on the Thought of Alfred North Whitehead*

*Living Options in Protestant Theology:
  A Survey of Methods*

Varieties of Protestantism

LIBERAL
CHRISTIANITY
AT THE
CROSSROADS

by JOHN B. COBB, JR.

THE WESTMINSTER PRESS · PHILADELPHIA

PUBLISHED BY THE WESTMINSTER PRESS ®
PHILADELPHIA, PENNSYLVANIA

PRINTED IN THE UNITED STATES OF AMERICA

Library of Congress Cataloging in Publication Data

Cobb, John B.
Liberal Christianity at the crossroads.

1. Liberalism (Religion) I. Title.
BR1615.C57   201'.1   73–9738
ISBN 0–664–20977–7

Contents

Preface

During the academic year 1972–1973 I have served as theologian-in-residence at the Church of the Crossroads in Honolulu. This congregation was founded fifty years ago as a liberal interracial church, conscious of the need for Christians to be open to the religious traditions of Asia. Because of its openness to fresh winds and currents, it has had a stormy history, experiencing in intensified form the passions and hopes that have flowed through liberal Protestantism generally. That has meant in recent years continuing interest in East Asia, active involvement with the counter-culture, opposition to the Vietnam war including giving sanctuary to deserters, and sponsorship of human potential programs. It has also meant an inner struggle with the ideas of secular Christianity, the church as mission, the death of God, and worship as celebration.

This book owes both its title and its content to the opportunity to work in this context. Most of these chapters are adapted from sermons preached here. Although the more obvious homiletical touches have been removed, along with most local references, the discerning reader will perceive traces of the sermonic origin. One of these traces is the relative autonomy of the chapters. Whereas in writing a book one usually builds explicitly upon the early chapters as he proceeds, a sermon must stand on its own feet and, in terms of its particular topic, communicate the gospel. The sermonic form remains in that each chapter ends on a note of grace, and there is very little explicit transition between chapters or reference from one chapter to another. Also, I have left untouched the extensive use of the first person plural pronoun.

I have tried in these chapters to share as a liberal Christian with other liberal Christians an understanding of where we are and where we are called to go. I am convinced that liberal Christianity has little future unless it can articulate its stance to itself in such a way as to differentiate itself from the activist, mystical, and psychological movements toward which it gravitates from time to time. Theologically it cannot exist as a watered-down form of conservative Christianity. If we liberal Christians are unable to state the authentic Christian gospel meaningfully and relevantly in our own terms, there is little value in our survival. Unless it is the Christian gospel that makes us liberal, and not simply an erosion of faith, we are not in any serious sense liberal Christians. I am personally troubled by the extent to which we have lost our centeredness in the gospel, but I remain quite sure that the gospel requires of us that we be liberal.

My particular perspective within liberal Christianity has been shaped by years of living with the philosophical vision of Alfred North Whitehead. The understanding of grace, which is the single most pervasive theme of these chapters, is derived from him, although the word is not his and he might have been surprised by this use of his thought.

This book is dedicated with gratitude and admiration to the Church of the Crossroads in honor of its fifty years of pioneering Christian service. May it dare to continue making mistakes when that is the price of blazing new trails!

J.B.C., Jr.

Honolulu

1

Liberal Christianity
at the Crossroads

At the time that I went to Hawaii, I decided to read James Michener's book on those islands. The dominant figure in the whole book is Abner Hale. He is undoubtedly a caricature of one side of the early missionary spirit, but he is, from the point of view of the story, a successful caricature. He embodies the spirit of traditional New England Calvinism in all its ambiguity. On the one hand he is devoted, dedicated, wholly self-sacrificial, utterly courageous in serving God as he understands the service of God. He is immensely successful in changing the character of a people. We cannot but admire him and resent the brutality of the captain who destroys his powers. On the other hand he is narrow, rigid, and intolerant, and from our point of view a racist, a bigot, and a fanatic. We do not like him.

Michener places as a foil to Hale the figure of John Whipple. Whipple too is a devoted Christian who comes to Hawaii with Hale as a medical missionary, but for Whipple faith is intertwined with common sense, openness to the values of other cultures, and a scientific understanding of his world. His tolerant spirit causes him to leave the mission, although he continues to place his medical knowledge at the service of others. We would like Whipple. But we should notice two things about him. First, he makes no comparable impact to that of Hale. Second, when he leaves the mission he enters business, and to success in business he gives something of the same ruthless devotion that Hale gives to the service of God.

Whipple represents for us the liberal Christian, genial and attractive, but lacking in commitment and power. His liberalism is the watering down of the substance of his faith which stems from historic Christianity.

The image I have chosen for the title of this chapter is an all too obvious one for church people in these times. Consider the crossroads at which we stand as liberal Christians in terms of decisiveness of commitment on the one hand and openness on the other.

We liberals have come down the road from historic Christianity progressively using up the capital of our heritage and doing little to replenish it. We have come more and more to mirror our culture, or certain strands within it, rather than to speak to it an effective word of judgment or healing. We do well to recognize that the liberal Christians of Germany became in the '30s the German Christians who could hail Hitler as a new savior.

At the crossroads we can choose the way to the theological right. In the years after World War I, Karl Barth, recognizing the bankruptcy of liberal Christianity, pioneered that road. He showed that the turn to the right theologically could support courageous movements to the left in the political and social spheres. When Hitler came to power it was Barth's followers in Germany who constituted themselves as the Confessing Church and continued to speak and act with courage in the face of the Nazi tyranny and the apostasy of so many other Christians.

Today some of our children, whom we have fed pablum in our liberal churches, are finding new life in evangelical and Pentecostal movements. Most of us cannot take these quite seriously, since they are so out of touch with the broader cultural and intellectual currents of our century. But as Barth has shown us, the turn to the right need not be naïve. It may be chosen out of the deep and informed conviction that in the chaos of our times we must recover our roots and a transcendent focus of shared commitment.

Even so, despite the power and value of what can be found on the road to the right, for many of us it is too late. We are committed to openness to the truth that comes from multiple traditions and new discoveries in the present and the future. We cannot reaffirm one tradition against the others. However valuable the symbols and memories of the Christian heritage, they can no longer encompass the whole to which we must be open. The road to the right involves a going back, in however sophisticated a form, and we are committed to going forward, open to all truth and value from whatever source it comes to us.

Hence we are more attracted to the road to the left than that to the theological right. That, too, is a well-traveled road. But the record of its travelers is not entirely inspiring. They begin with a commitment to openness wherever it may lead. But commitment to openness as such does not provide a place to stand, a place from which to evaluate the many claimants for our attention and belief. Hence the road to the left leads to one of two ends. One may adopt the academic stance of openness to all and commitment to none. We professors especially, in our zeal to be open and fair, may present to our students a cafeteria of options, each with its strengths and weaknesses, while committing ourselves to none and growing gradually jaded by the whole affair. Alternately, openness may lead to the full acceptance of some vital and persuasive movement or vision, an acceptance that engrafts one into a new history but ends the openness to which he was first committed. For decades liberal Christian churches have supplied the universities with uncommitted intellectuals and each new social and cultural movement with many of its most dedicated followers. This is not a shameful record, but it shows that the road to the left holds little promise for the future.

The image of the crossroads, unlike that of a fork in the road, suggests that there is a third way we can go. Straight ahead. But whereas the roads to the right and the left are easy to make out and have well-known destinations, the road ahead is more like a goat path up a steep mountain. Only a few Christian thinkers have explored that trail, and their reports are conflicting. We do not know whether at the top we may reach a new plateau for travel or only more rugged cliffs. Even so, I am convinced that as liberal Christians we are called to scale the slope ahead.

We cannot do this if our liberal openness and our Christian commitment continue to be in tension with each other. Openness can be sustained only where it is grounded in a faith that justifies and requires it. But we can affirm Christian faith wholeheartedly today only insofar as it opens us to all truth and value. Openness and faith must be brought for us into a new relation of mutual support.

To sustain openness we need to say to every claimant on our appreciation and loyalty both yes and no. Unless we say yes, we will not be open to its truth and value. Unless we say no, our openness to that one claimant will close us to others. In other words, openness can be sustained only as we see all things as partial and fragmentary embodiments of a truth and goodness that they do not exhaust, so that when they claim for themselves completeness or finality, they deceive.

It is particularly important that we recognize this about ourselves individually, and about every community to which we belong. Openness requires continual self-criticism and continual social criticism especially of those movements with which we identify ourselves most closely.

In saying what is required in order that openness be sustained, I have been describing the prophetic principle, so close to the heart of our Judeo-Christian tradition. The prophets denounced their own people, not because they were worse than their neighbors, but because they failed to recognize the "more" that they were called to be. They denounced the rites and ceremonies of their times, not because they were evil, but because their observance made people complacent in the face of social injustices. Jesus denounced the Pharisees, not because they were the worst people of their time, but because they were the best, and just for that reason most likely to be closed to the new possibilities he proclaimed.

The prophetic principle thus grounds the openness we need. But can we affirm it? It is intimately bound up with a picture of a transcendent Lord of history that does not fit with our contemporary vision. The criticism it demands destroys that picture and every other picture of God. Against every theism it protests so as to produce a new atheism. But against every atheism, too, it must protest. Today as much as ever we can and must believe that truth and goodness stand beyond every personal and historical embodiment. In the name of that truth and goodness we can and must be critical of the best that we have and think so as to be open to that which we cannot yet have and think. That criticism and that openness are part of what it means to believe in God as faithful Christians in our time.

But there is another difficulty about this liberal Christian life. It is exhilarating, but it is also exhausting. Constant self-criticism alone cannot constitute our existence. None of us is strong enough for that.

Reinhold Niebuhr once said that the function of preaching is to afflict the comfortable and to comfort the afflicted. To afflict the comfortable is rather easy. I am afflicted again each time I pick up a newspaper, not just because of the suffering and injustice it reports, but also because of my sense of deep complicity in it. The prophetic principle is at work in me, and in our worship together it needs to be renewed and sharpened lest its edge be dulled. But I cannot endure to live only in that tension and guilt. What word can we say to comfort the afflicted? That is much harder.

We used to say, "While we were yet sinners, Christ died for us," and God so loved us "that he gave his only begotten Son." Luther and Calvin insisted that salvation is a wholly free gift, so that men should have no anxiety about meriting it. I for one believe that there is a strange truth in all that. But the rhetoric is not ours. It is our task together to find ways to mediate comfort to one another in our several and continuing afflictions. We need each other most of all here. To find the way of supporting and sustaining each other in the midst of our openness and self-criticism without glibness and sentimentality—that is not easy. But we can do it, for the truth and goodness that judge us comfort us as well.

2

Does It Matter?

Thucydides' history of the Peloponnesian War is one of the great books of all time. In it Athens appears as a tragic hero. Her faults are not concealed from us, and we know from the first the inevitability of her defeat. We even see that there may be more justice in Sparta's cause. But we side with Athens. The Athenian people embody so much of the spirit we admire—a spirit of creativity, love of beauty, self-reliance, and, to a degree, democracy. In their midst were some of the great artists and thinkers of all time.

One incident in the story struck me with peculiar painfulness when I first read the book many years ago and has remained in my memory. It is the story of Mytilene. Mytilene was a member of the confederacy of free cities that Athens gradually transformed into an empire. As in many such cities the common people were sympathetic to Athens, whereas the oligarchy resented Athens and preferred an alliance with Sparta. Under the rule of the oligarchy Mytilene revolted against Athens, counting on Spartan aid. The Spartan fleet, however, was slow in coming, whereas the Athenians came promptly. To defend themselves the Mytileneans armed the common people, who then insisted on making terms with the Athenians. The city surrendered on the single condition that before it was punished the case would be heard by the citizens of Athens. The Athenians were furious that in a time of war a member of the confederacy would turn against them. They voted to kill all the men of the city and to sell the women and children into slavery.

I am glad to say that this story has a relatively happy ending. The people of Athens repented of their decision. The next day they reassembled and reversed themselves. They dispatched fast ships which arrived just in time to stay the slaughter. Only the leaders were executed.

When I first read the story, what struck me with painful force was the fact that the great and free people of Periclean Athens could publicly and collectively decide on so cruel and unjust a punishment. On rereading the story recently, I was more struck by the fact that they changed their minds.

What has happened to me in the intervening years is that I have participated in the widespread American experience of the loss of innocence. Twenty-five years ago, although I might verbally have denied it, I inwardly felt that I was part of a nation incapable of cruelty of such dimensions. Of course I knew that the United States had done some morally questionable things, but I viewed all of them as secondary to a fundamentally virtuous history. I wanted the United States to become more fully involved in world affairs on the assumption that it would exercise its power basically for justice and peace and the economic development of other peoples. I could not understand how the Athenian people, so like us in many ways, could have been capable of such egregious cruelty.

But the past two decades have forced us to re-view our history. We must see it through the eyes of Indians and blacks and Orientals and Mexicans, and it is transformed into a story of greed and exploitation, racism and nationalism, all papered over with a transparently hypocritical rhetoric.

We could come to terms emotionally with this new picture of our distant past if we could see our recent experience in a different light. But alas. In recent times, we have given our support to dictatorships in Greece and Portugal and Brazil and have opposed creative reform in Guatemala, Cuba, the Dominican Republic, and in Chile. And above all, there has been our destructive involvement in Vietnam.

We might like to claim that the American people are not responsible for the crimes in Vietnam. By a substantial majority we wanted to get out and leave Vietnam to the Vietnamese. But alas this position was not taken on moral grounds. Once the pressure of the draft was removed, the resistance to the war on college campuses eroded. Once the American casualty list declined, the level of protest against the destruction of Vietnamese lives dropped drastically. Most Americans would have liked to win the war regardless of the moral considerations involved. It was only when we saw that we could not win that we favored extrication. By a considerable majority we supported Nixon's thoroughly amoral policies.

Many of us, when we realize how deeply we are implicated in the raw use of power to achieve immoral ends, react with anger. We will not tolerate this. We have a democracy in which we can make our voices heard. We organize to change our national policy.

So we tried for many years to stop this vicious and seemingly endless war in Southeast Asia. But we failed. We made headway in one place, only to find that we had lost ground in another.

Furthermore, we found our efforts caught up in a web of ambiguities. To achieve political success we simplified the issues to the point of falsification. We pretended that there were easier solutions than in fact existed. We portrayed those who disagreed with us as fools or as wicked conspirators. We belittled the element of betrayal of allies that would be involved in extricating ourselves. We employed means that involved the violation of laws, and we resented those who pointed out the moral questionableness of such means and were shocked when our efforts backfired against our cause. Our motives were a tangle of concern for the Vietnamese and for our own self-image as righteous people. The net result of all our efforts was that in place of our infantry killing Vietnamese one by one, our nation automated battlefields and instituted mass bombing.

Involved in such abortive efforts, we become more frustrated. From time to time we find new channels by which to vent our anger in constructive, if still ambiguous, ways; but on the whole we find ourselves instead on the verge of despair. In the face of a reality that matters deeply to us, and with full recognition of its horrible moral evil, we find ourselves impotent, and we cannot even take satisfaction in the purity of our own motives and acts. To understand ourselves in relation to such a history is deeply disillusioning.

If we cannot find meaning in history, where shall we turn? One possibility is to take a larger, evolutionary view. Perhaps in the play of seemingly meaningless forces can be discerned a meaning on the larger scale that is invisible in current events.

The most powerful contemporary vision of such a meaning is that of Teilhard de Chardin. In the total history of life on our planet he saw our time as the beginning of a great convergence of all men into a new and ultimate redemptive unity of mutual enrichment. Even in the totalitarian collectivisms of the '30s and the great war of the '40s he was able to discern movement toward what he called the Omega. Certainly it is the case that over the eons we can discern a growth and progress that is not apparent when we judge instead in terms of recent historical epochs. If we can derive no meaning for our lives from our involvement in the immediate events of history, perhaps we can endow them with significance as a part of an overarching movement toward a distant consummation.

There are two problems with this. First, in spite of all Teilhard's careful qualifications, the Christian must fear that when the eye is set on so distant a horizon, it will be too easy to neglect the urgent cry of the neighbor for food and justice. The evolutionary scale of millions of years threatens to diminish the importance of the cup of cold water to the thirsty man.

Second, many of us can no longer have confidence in an evolutionary future. Teilhard, in his last years, wrestled with the problem of man's new technical power of self-destruction. But he convinced himself that man would not use it. Now, however, we realize that to destroy ourselves we need only continue in the way we are already going.

I heard a simple story once about a tiny island covered with grass. Sailors stopped there for water and noticed that there were no animals. How perfect, they thought, for rabbits; so they released a few, planning to come back later for fresh meat. When they returned a few years later, however, they found the island littered with the corpses of rabbits. They had multiplied unchecked in that rabbit paradise until, abruptly, they exhausted the food. Then they starved. We now are too much like those rabbits cheerfully multiplying our numbers and our consumption with abundant resources. Only, unlike rabbits, we can foresee the danger. But if we do, then the distant horizon is no longer reassuring. It is imminent historical actions that will determine whether there can be any long-term future at all. Omega may beckon, but it will not save us. So we are thrown back into the cycle of activism and frustration and despair.

If, then, we are to find meaning, we seem to be driven back to the smaller sphere of our family, our friends, and our inner lives. In small groups, kindness and mutual concern sometimes prevail over raw power, and here and now we can find satisfaction in exploring the mysteries of the psyche and in opening ourselves to each other. If history is driven by inexorable forces, and if we can have no confidence in an ultimate consummation of the evolutionary process, then must we not seek meaning here?

The problem is that we cannot shut ourselves off from the currents of history even in our sensitivity and meditation groups or in our families. Our efforts to escape history are an expression of our historical situation. And that changing situation breaks in upon our lives inevitably and continuously. If history is amoral and meaningless, then, in the end, so is every aspect of our lives.

What, then, shall we do? When we seek the meaning of our lives in participation in history, we are driven to despair. But

when we seek to overcome this despair by expanding the scale
to that of evolution or contracting it to intimate relations we find
ourselves thrown back upon history.

We have two choices. The first is to root out of our very
beings all sense of meaning and morality. This sense is not easily
exorcised, for it is the product of three thousand years of Judeo-
Christian history. But we cannot live in despair, and for a hundred years many sensitive Westerners have been coming to
terms with the possibility of a history and a personal life without
morality and without meaning. To the question, "Does it matter?" they have learned to say, "No."

They have learned to see history as a field of power struggle
in which moral ideals are in fact only weapons in the hands of
the antagonists. Those with power always use their power to
exploit the powerless, and they always will. They believe that
to accept man and his world is to accept *this* man and *this* world.
To moralize about it is only to create misery in yourself and
others. There is much that is attractive in this view.

Richard Rubenstein, the rabbi who wrote the book *After
Auschwitz,* has argued that after the horrors perpetrated against
the European Jews under Hitler it is no longer possible to believe
in the Judeo-Christian God, for to believe in God is to believe
that Auschwitz too has meaning. In that book and in some of his
other utterances there was an understandable bitterness against
Christians and Christianity. But when Rubenstein rejected belief
in God he moved toward an amoral view of history. Once the
Jews were driven out of Israel by the Romans, he now believes,
Auschwitz became inevitable. Events are governed by inexorable
historical forces, not by morality. Hence it is pointless to accuse
and to excuse. For the Christian, at least, this nonjudgmental
Rubenstein is easier to take than the accusing prophet.

William Golding, author of *Lord of the Flies,* tells the story in
The Inheritors of the meeting of Cro-Magnon with Neanderthal
man. The story is told from the point of view of the more primitive, less aggressive, Neanderthal man. It is a horrible but all too
plausible account of his destruction. It is a parable of what has

always happened in history when a more advanced people encounter a less advanced and, usually, less warlike one. Perhaps we can have more compassion for our ancestors for their treatment of Africans and Indians if we realize that this is part of a universal pattern rather than an expression of peculiar viciousness on their part.

Perhaps, in the reading of the past, an amoral view has much to commend it. But our reading of the past will carry over into our reading of the present and undercut our passion for justice and our hope that men can even now rise above raw power in their treatment of one another. Perhaps we can come to terms with the exploitations of the past, but should we complacently stand aside as the sacred mountain of the Navajos is strip-mined and the ecology of their region destroyed in order to produce more electricity to meet the insatiable demands of us Californians? Should we simply accept as inevitable the continued slaughter of the primitive Indians of the Amazon because they are felt to be a nuisance by the new developers and builders of roads?

There are tough-minded people who have learned to accept the exploitation and genocide that are occurring in our time without flinching and without moral judgment. These too they see as products of the inexorable forces of history.

Albert Camus thought in this way at one point in his life. He had a German friend with whom he talked about what this viewpoint implied. The friend went on to become a Nazi. Camus found deep within himself that he did not, could not, believe that this amoral view of life was the last word. Toward the end of World War II he wrote his friend as follows:

"For a long time we both thought that this world had no ultimate meaning. . . . I still think so in a way. But I came to different conclusions from the ones you used to talk about, which, for so many years now, you have been trying to introduce into history. I tell myself now that if I had really followed your reasoning, I ought to approve what you are doing. . . .

"You never believed in the meaning of this world, and you

therefore deduced the idea that everything was equivalent and
that good and evil could be defined according to one's wishes.
. . . You concluded that . . . the only pursuit for the individual was the adventure of power and his only morality, the
realism of conquests. And, to tell the truth, I, believing I thought
as you did, saw no valid argument to answer you except a fierce
love of justice which, after all, seemed to me as unreasonable as
the most sudden passion. . . .

". . . From the same principle we derived quite different
codes. . . . You chose injustice and sided with the gods. . . .

"I, on the contrary, chose justice in order to remain faithful
to the world. I continue to believe that this world has no ultimate
meaning. But I know that something in it has a meaning and
that is man, because he is the only creature to insist on having
one. . . . With your scornful smile you will ask me: what do
you mean by saving man? And with all my being I shout to you
that I mean not mutilating him and yet giving a chance to the
justice that man alone can conceive." (Albert Camus, *Resistance, Rebellion, and Death,* tr. by Justin O'Brien [Alfred A.
Knopf, Inc., 1961], pp. 27f.)

Camus could not root out of his being the sense of meaning
and morality, however narrowly he was forced to circumscribe
the former. Like him, in spite of ourselves, we find meaning in
a moral response to history. Camus cried out that it does matter
what happens. However frustrated we become, however strongly
despair threatens, we are not finally allowed to believe that it
does not matter. Instead, we must learn to see that *everything*
matters.

Everything matters—there is no rest for us. There will always
be new claims upon our attention, new demands for help, as
long as we live. To cease to recognize those claims is to be inwardly dead.

Because everything matters, we are forever denied self-
satisfaction. We must face the endless perversity of our motives
and the inevitable ambiguity of all our actions.

But because everything matters, we can endure without rest

and without self-satisfaction. *We* matter as individuals. Our every hope and fear, our angry and generous feelings, our little gestures for good and ill—all are important. We are people of worth. To realize that in the depths of our beings is to know the blessing and affirmation of God.

3

The Story We Live

The public schools have been a major center of controversy. It is right and inevitable that this be so. We all pay taxes to support them, and most of us send our children to them to be educated. We cannot or should not be indifferent to how our children are educated.

Today the controversy centers on busing, and this is a special and highly ambiguous form of the deeper controversy as to whether our children should be grouped in schools according to ethnic, cultural, and economic status. That is an important issue. Controversies flare up from time to time also over sex education, the way children are taught to read, the observance of Christian holidays, prayer in the classroom, and the teaching of evolution.

Less frequently the dispute goes into more substantive matters of the content of texts and courses. Here controversy focuses most often on the teaching of history and, especially, of American history. That focus expresses a sound instinct. A major function of our public schools, alongside teaching the three "R's," has been the Americanization of children from diverse backgrounds. The central means of that Americanization is the teaching of American history. How we understand ourselves as Americans is a function of how we read that history. The Birch Society is right, from its point of view, to be concerned about the element of self-criticism that some of our American histories have recently contained. Blacks and Mexicans and Jews and Indians and Orientals are right to be concerned about the way they are pictured or ignored in the story.

One might argue that in the writing of history we should be concerned only for truth—not for the interests of special groups. But that is to misunderstand history as story. The past is inexhaustibly complex. Even if a group of people should limit themselves to a consideration of the events occurring in a fifteen-minute period in a particular room, and everyone should cooperate for the rest of their lives in seeking to report them accurately, they would touch on only a very small portion of these events in highly selected ways. Their sentences would never exhaust the actuality.

To tell a story is to select, abstract, arrange, and interpret. Hence it involves distortion. The story never corresponds to what it is about. There can be many equally true stories of the same events.

This variety of true stories was brought home to me in grade school. I attended a Canadian school in Japan. There in alternate years we studied Canadian history from a Canadian textbook, British history from a British textbook, and United States history from an American textbook. For the most part they dealt with quite different events, but they were most interesting where they overlapped.

All three dealt with the American Revolution. The Canadian history told of the heroic defense of the Canadians against the brutal efforts of the colonies to the south to force them into disloyalty. It told also of the influx of loyal British subjects who were being persecuted in the rebellious colonies. The British history gave only a paragraph or two to the event. It was portrayed as a side issue to the great wars raging in Europe. The British decided that it was not worth the trouble to suppress the rebellion. I need not tell you of the stories of brilliant exploits against great odds which filled whole chapters of the American history.

All these accounts were true, but of course they all offered highly selected and distorted truths. Each was written from a particular perspective governed by particular interests and questions. Any history must be. Equally every perspective on the past and present is shaped by some reading of the past.

How we have viewed our alternatives in Vietnam has been largely shaped by our perception of American history. For example, if we read American history as the expansion from thirteen weak and disunited colonies to world dominance in service of a mission to spread throughout the world the enlightened American way of democracy, equal opportunity, and prosperity through competition, then we will think that what was above all important in Vietnam was that we not falter because of petty moral scruples but do whatever was necessary to impose our will upon that land. Whereas if we read American history as the struggle to subordinate power to justice and moderate justice by mercy, then we would see in our behavior in Vietnam an appalling failure of our true calling and would long to share in public confession and repentance.

That the struggle about the present is at the same time a struggle over the reading of the past is nothing new. Indeed, it is characteristic of the whole Judeo-Christian tradition. The New Testament provides us with many good illustrations, for example, the question of how to interpret the event of Jesus' death on the cross. The background for interpretation is given by the Scriptures, that is, by the history of Israel. But how is that history to be read? Christian preaching in the early days consisted to a large degree of retelling that story so as to show that the crucified Jesus was the messiah of Israel. The Jews who rejected Jesus continued to tell it, of course, in another way. To this day a major difference between Jews and Christians is the way each reads Israel's story. In general, Jews read it in terms of the law, with the prophets playing a secondary role. Christians read it in terms of the prophets, with the law playing a secondary role.

At first, the Christian story was told for Jews. As Christianity grew among the Gentiles, however, it was told and retold to make sense of this unexpected development. In Rom., chs. 9 to 11, we find Paul's most sustained effort to carry forward the Christian story so as to include and interpret these events. In some of the later New Testament writings, such as Revelation, the persecutions suffered by the Christians at the hands of the Romans were given meaning by a further extension of the story. And in *The City of God* the greatest of Christian theologians, Augustine, retold the story of the world so as to make sense of the whole history of the Roman Empire that was crumbling around him.

In modern times, however, few have lived by these ancient Christian stories. Beginning in the Renaissance and winning dominance in the Enlightenment was a quite different story in which the civilization of Greece and Rome constituted the focus of interest and the period of Christian triumph in the Middle Ages was deprecated. The tellers of this story gradually gained more confidence in their own time until, in their accounts, classical antiquity faded into the background and the modern world rose to dominance as the bearer of light and progress. These histories could then portray the exploration, conquest, and settlement of the rest of the planet by Europeans together with their growing science and technology and new social and political institutions as the basis of interpreting events and guiding the course of current affairs. Social Darwinism in the writing of history, together with images of the white man's burden and manifest destiny and bringing the Kingdom of God, gave meaning to life in the half century leading up to World War I.

Those histories are to us now just as alien as the Biblical and Augustinian ones. Where does that leave us?

This is an acute question for professional historians and philosophers of history. In general, they have abandoned the effort to write universal history. They content themselves with bits and pieces of specialized inquiry into the past. They try to throw light not on our present existence in general but rather on some limited aspect of it. Nevertheless, they are caught in a dilemma.

As long as they deal with meaningful interpretation at all, they are involved with presuppositions which, if examined, will point back toward some implicit view of universal history and the relation of their narrow subjects to it. If they abandon the quest for meaningful interpretation, then they must recognize their own efforts as trivia not worth the attention of serious men.

If professional historians refuse to tell us a story about the human past to illumine the present, we may be sure that others, less fastidious, and less well qualified, will supply the lack. Christian fundamentalists tell the story of man's creation, fall, and redemption, and point forward to a final judgment. Marxists tell how bourgeois society rises from a feudal past and bears within itself the seeds of its own destruction and of the rise of a communist society. Nietzsche describes the death of God and the coming of the superior man. Charles Reich pictures our time as that of the rise of "Consciousness III" against the background of "Consciousness I" and "Consciousness II." Norman Brown portrays civilization as rising on the basis of repression and now to be overthrown by the liberation of the body. Meanwhile white supremacists, Black Muslims, Latin revolutionists, Palestinian guerrillas, Israelis, and many others are telling their stories with passionate conviction as a basis for present action.

Many of these stories are interesting and enlightening. None of them are wholly false. We are moved by each. But as liberal Christians we distance ourselves critically from all of them. The truth of one too often conflicts with the truth of the others. The factual errors and cruder distortions of interpretations involved in each offend our love of truth, but our criticisms appear as petty and irrelevant to those who live by these stories. They attack us as uncommitted spectators incapable of effective action.

The criticism hurts because it seems true. In comparison with the dedication of Black Muslims and Palestinian guerrillas, our gestures seem frivolous. Apparently we do not believe in anything strongly enough to live and die for it. We sadly watch while those less troubled by questions of objective truth and fairness become the only real actors on the scene.

There is much truth in that picture of ourselves, but it is not the whole truth. Our reaction to the criticism shows that we too implictly live by a story that calls for action. Otherwise we would be indifferent to the charge. Our recognition of the selective truth and the distortions of these many stories shows that our story is a more inclusive one. Our ability to respond positively to all the other stories shows that ours deals with more fundamental values.

Perhaps if we can uncover and articulate our own inchoate story we can both be more critical of the judgments we pass upon others and more effective as participants in history. Perhaps we can learn to tell that story with conviction, in spite of our acknowledgment that it is too fragmentary and selective.

The story by which we live is correlative with the values we prize. It is the story of the rise of life out of the inanimate, and of consciousness out of the unconscious. It traces the emergence out of the pre-human of the human and of the distinctively human capacities for language, for humor, for worship, for art, and for thought. It recounts the use of these capacities, on the one hand, for destruction and conquest and, on the other, for bringing about order and justice on a broadening scale. It notes the rise of an understanding which assigns worth to the individual and hence to all individuals and thus challenges the absolute right of the group to impose its collective will. The story portrays the emergence of a love of truth for truth's sake and its struggle against the myths and ideologies by which men justify their self-interested actions. It finds here and there a concern of men for other men that goes beyond the erotic. It presents the development of visions of the future that include all men in a world of peace, justice, and mutual affection.

The story shows, however, all these changes against a background in which in the great course of events might too often triumphs over right. Those who have hold of partial truths often destroy each other for the sake of those truths and the institutions developed to preserve and enlarge the scope of love often become instruments in self-aggrandizement. The struggle that matters most is fought out, not between good people and bad people, but within the heart of each man. Men are capable of endless self-deception, so that the emergence of every ideal becomes an occasion for hypocrisy. Those who pursue truth most vigorously and those who love justice most passionately often become most cynical. Through the story we see our time both as one of vast achievement and potential and as one in which men have lost confidence that the achievement is worthwhile or the potential actualizable.

This story by which we live is a universal one, to be traced in its distinctiveness in every culture. It finds its richest expressions in those two great families of cultures which we call East and West. Our century is one of decisive interpenetration of those two cultures. How that interpenetration occurs will determine the cultural and human possibilities for the next century. Liberal Christians, open to both East and West, have an opportunity for creative leadership in the deepest events of our time. The chapter of the story that we now write can be as great as any.

I have spoken of the history by which the liberal Christian lives without reference to Jesus, but in fact Jesus has dominated all that I have said. We read history as we do because we are the products of a history at whose center he stands. It is a history that is fed by many streams that have not flowed through him, but our openness to those streams and our selective acceptance of their contributions are because of him. That we seek to understand our present through an inclusive story of the past we owe to him.

To realize that Jesus is the center of the history in which we find meaning for our lives now can liberate us from false attempts to prove our devotion to him. We do not have to bring Jesus artificially into our rhetoric or attempt to force our lives into a pattern that we associate with him. We do not need to whip up strong emotions about him or about his crucifixion for our sake. We do not need to employ the language about him that has characterized our tradition. But we do need honestly to recognize that what is most important and precious in our lives we owe to a history of which he is the hinge. The attempt to understand ourselves more fully and more critically will then lead us to seek a clearer understanding of him as well. But in the process we are called, not to put on a special pair of supposedly Christian glasses, but to use our eyes as they are, to call the shots as we see them, to give ourselves to those causes which commend themselves to us under whatever label.

To find the meaning of our lives through Jesus is to be free. We do not have to struggle for that freedom. We need only to recognize and to accept what is true before we seek it. The story by which we live has already set us free.

4

Jesus the Disturber

Jesus is the most important figure in world history. Superficially this is attested by the worldwide acceptance of a system of dating in which the supposed year of his birth marks the inauguration of our age. But there are much deeper reasons for this affirmation.

Most history these days is written from a quite secular point of view in which the religious foundation of culture is little understood or appreciated. Even so, accounts of the events in Europe through the sixteenth and seventeenth centuries are filled with testimony to the importance of Christian institutions and indirectly of Jesus. As one reads on, the church plays a lesser and lesser role, so that the student of European, and even American, history might suppose that the church had almost disappeared as a significant factor by the nineteenth century.

However, the myopia of these historical accounts is already apparent. In retrospect from the present we must judge that the changes taking place in the nineteenth century among Asian and African peoples were more important than most of the political squabbles in Europe that have dazzled our historians. And if we ask how these changes came about, the most accurate simple answer is that the peoples of Asia and Africa came into contact with that great disturber, Jesus.

We must recognize that it was as disturber and not as savior in some other sense that Jesus played his dominant role in the nineteenth century. There are, of course, Christian churches throughout Asia and Africa that bear witness to other dimensions of his impact as well. But far beyond the walls of these new churches the encounter with Jesus aroused dissatisfaction with a *status quo* which men had previously regarded as natural or inevitable and to which they had been resigned. In the light of Jesus, the injustice and unacceptability of both the traditional social structures and the new colonialism became apparent. The restlessness and criticism awakened by Jesus gave birth to the great nationalist and socialist revolutions of the twentieth century that have dramatically changed the map of the world and reduced Western Europe to one among half a dozen centers of power. Even in the nineteenth century, unnoticed by our historians, Jesus was the most important figure in world history.

That Jesus is the most important figure in world history is more readily acknowledged by thinkers who are accustomed to looking behind social and political changes to the grounds from which they spring. In Eastern Europe a good many Marxist intellectuals today are extremely interested in Christianity, because they recognize that Marxism deals only with a segment of life and requires a wider and a deeper context in the understanding of man. Many of them would recognize that Jesus, rather than Marx, is the center of history. Thoughtful Hindus and Buddhists recognize how much of their contemporary self-understanding has grown out of their encounter and competition with Christianity, especially in India and Japan. The Christian challenge has extricated the fundamental religious impulse in their life from the cultural and traditional patterns in which it was immersed. Even the great enemies of Christianity, such as Friedrich Nietzsche, recognized in Jesus the one adversary worthy of all their efforts.

Some who recognize that the Crucified One towers over all other figures in world history deplore it. But we, as Christians, rejoice, regretting only that his influence is so often corruptly

mediated by his followers. When we acknowledge Jesus as the
center of *our* history, we make not only a judgment about the
facts but also a confession of evaluation. What has come to us
from him is that in terms of which we interpret and evaluate
what we receive from other sources as well. That we are self-
critical at all, and the particular way in which we criticize ourselves, derives from Jesus.

If this is so, then we must recognize that our relation to Jesus
is of utmost importance for us, that to be more nearly what we
would be is to perfect that relation. But when we then undertake
to perfect that relation, either we do so naïvely and pietistically
or we find that we confront difficult questions, many of which
had hardly occurred to us.

We cannot improve our relation to Jesus unless we know who
he was. For example, if he was a teacher who expounded enduring moral and spiritual laws, then to improve our relation to
him would be to believe what he taught and to obey the laws
he showed us. If he was a perfect personality embodying the
ideal form of humanity to which all aspire, then we should seek
to be more like him. If he was one who pointed away from himself to God or to the Kingdom of God, then we should look with
him at what he saw. If he was one who denied the importance
of the world and all that takes place within it in the name of
another world, then we should practice asceticism.

Liberal Christians in the nineteenth century felt the importance of these questions and devoted remarkable scholarly gifts,
motivated by deep Christian passion, to finding the answers.
Albert Schweitzer has commented that their work and their
achievements were unique in human history. To this day no
other religious community has criticized its sacred scriptures so
ruthlessly, with such a commitment to truth. But the quest failed.
Schweitzer himself wrote the obituary. The failure of the quest
must warn us as to the extent to which the Jesus to whom we
try to relate is likely to be more the product of our fancies than
the man who once lived in Galilee.

Less dramatically the quest has been renewed in the twentieth century. New methods of historical inquiry have been forged. Gradually the pendulum swing from theory to theory has become less wild, and a small body of reliable results has emerged. These tell us little of Jesus' personality. They do not enable us to explain the sequence of events in his ministry or any development in his thought. They indicate very little concerning what view he may have had of himself or what his motives may have been. But they do allow us to say some things about Jesus' message and about how he characteristically acted.

Perhaps what we can say with greatest confidence is that he was—and is—a disturbing figure. We can be quite sure that he included tax collectors in the community meals that were so central to his life with his disciples. That would be like a Norwegian during the Nazi occupation throwing parties for Quisling and his associates—only more so, for the common meal meant far more in Jesus' day than a party could mean in occupied Norway. We can be sure also that he overturned reasonable conceptions of justice, as in the parable of the laborers in the vineyard (Matt. 20:1–16), where those who worked only a few minutes were paid as much as those who worked all day.

The Jewish leaders of Jesus' day could not assimilate such action and such teaching into their understanding of goodness. Neither can we, even though we have the advantage of being able to understand his teaching historically. That is, we can see that the ground of his strange behavior and stories was his conviction that God's Kingdom was breaking in, that the decision each man made in relation to that Kingdom set aside all other considerations. We, on the other hand, know that world history continued and continues. Hence our judgments can and must be made in the context of this ongoingness rather than in that of the imminence of the end of history.

It might seem, then, that we should just dismiss Jesus as a deluded fanatic. But we can't. Something happened when he turned the world upside down. Men saw their lives in a new and very disturbing light. It was disturbing because on the one hand it showed them things about themselves that, once having seen, they could not forget, whereas on the other hand there was no adjustment of their lives which could comfortably reconcile them to this new truth. We are still caught in that quandary. For example, when we are told that prostitutes are better than preachers, how do we react? We preachers would like to ridicule the idea, but we cannot. It has a haunting truth that will not let us go. Should we, then, encourage everyone to become a prostitute? Of course not. That would be totally to misunderstand Jesus. It was in repentance that the prostitute showed her superiority. Should we, then, confess the preachers' sins of pride and hardheartedness and vested interest in established patterns that become apparent to us as we hear Jesus' condemnation? Of course, but having confessed, we are not off the hook. We are still enmeshed in the habits of feeling, thought, and action whose bondage we have admitted.

To come to terms with Jesus has been throughout the centuries an immensely disturbing challenge to Christians. We can distinguish four main ways in which we have attempted it.

The Catholic Church rightly saw that the demands of Jesus were unreasonable and inappropriate for the ordinary man who must support a family and carry on the affairs of the world. For him the church taught a stringent but practical morality derived from the Old Testament and Stoicism. The distinctively Christian element in his life came through the sacraments by means of which Christ became redemptively present to him. Those, however, who could not settle for this halfway house, those who wanted to be fully Christian, separated themselves from the world. For them the church institutionalized the religious life. This involved renunciation of sex and property and the control of one's own life so that he could live in the upside-down world of the gospel.

Through the centuries there has been another, a sectarian, response. It was contemptuous of the Catholic solution. In the sectarian view there can be no halfway Christianity. Every Christian is called to full discipleship to this disturbing Jesus. Each must live out this discipleship in the world with the responsibilities entailed in raising a family. In just that context he must renounce all use of force, turn the other cheek when affronted, and give his last garment to whoever asks for it.

Of course, governments cannot function on such radical principles. And some Christians believed that living in the world required participation in shaping the course of events rather than passive response alone. Luther struggled with this problem, rejecting monasticism with the sectarians but seeking to affirm an ethic of the possible with the Catholics. Luther saw that even the monks and the sectarians who strove for perfection did not attain it, that they were constantly falling under Jesus' condemnation of the Pharisees for self-deception and self-righteousness. None, he was convinced, could live by Jesus' teaching. But that excused none from living in continual relation to that teaching. It was Jesus who once and for all made clear that no man is righteous, that no man can save himself, and that we are wholly dependent on grace.

Christians influenced by Romanticism questioned the intense focus on continuing sinfulness of the Lutheran view. They were concerned to emphasize the fulfillment of human potentialities and the possibility of bringing into being a more Christian society. They found in Jesus a high appraisal of man as man, the infinite worth of the individual, and the vision of a society in which God's will is done on earth. Jesus as companion and helper on our upward journey replaced Jesus the disturber. But Jesus has refused this role. He remains the abrasive teacher who turns all things upside down.

All these responses to Jesus have their saints and heroes. Each has penetrated deeply into the hearts and minds of many Christians and has shaped churches and social institutions that endure to our own time. But none has succeeded finally—or at least, none has succeeded for us.

We find ourselves again in confrontation with Jesus the disturber, who will not let us rest even in our best responses to him. As we look at him we find ourselves lifted and borne forward by a history in which his spirit, often incognito, has remained the driving force. But we see that even the best embodiments of that spirit, whether churches, schools, or revolutionary movements, are extremely ambiguous. In the direct light of Jesus' teaching they appear to us as corrupt and corrupting. We find ourselves entangled in the corruption, in the inertia, in the hypocrisy, and in the self-deceit and halfheartedness of life. But unlike Jesus and some of our Christian forebears, we see no way out. No Kingdom is now breaking in to free the world from ambiguity and suffering. We are called to live in this world without pretending to purity of heart, never satisfied, always seeking ways to deal with particular problems, but without the illusion that our efforts will usher in an age when effort will no longer be needed. We must give ourselves unstintingly to causes likely to fail, causes whose success would only open the way to new problems. To respond to Jesus in this way is not to escape the disturbing recognition of the inadequacy of the response. Yet it is to some such response as this that we are called.

Fortunately there is another side to the teaching of Jesus in addition to the insatiable demand. The extremeness of his call is matched by the extremeness of his promise. God forgives without limit and without conditions. He is more ready to give than we are to seek. God's present action in the world is there to be experienced with joy.

The grounds of Jesus' promise are the same as the grounds of his demand—the inbreaking Kingdom of God. Those grounds are not ours today. But just as the demands continue to disturb us even when we do not share their grounds, so also the promises continue to assure us even though we cannot believe them in the form they take in Jesus. We continue to struggle for a goodness that will allow us to approve of ourselves. And that goodness, in the light of Jesus, always eludes us. But just at the point of deepest disgust with ourselves, our pretensions, and our defenses, we find a paradoxical affirmation. We are forgiven, and therefore forgive ourselves. Just when our efforts to forge ahead collapse, we find ourselves borne forward and set upright again.

The upside-downness of the world into which we are thrown

by Jesus the disturber turns out also to reverse our misery as well. Just as our greatest successes are turned into failure, so also our failure is turned into success. Just as our joy is turned into wretchedness, so also is our wretchedness turned into joy.

The world that Jesus gives us is one we cannot manage or control. The worlds that we understand and organize all collapse at his touch even when they are constructed in his name. That does not free us from the responsibility of constructing such worlds or of forming them in service to him. But when we have accepted the fact that he destroys all that we do even, and especially, when we do it in his name, then we are ready for the joyful surprise that the destruction is blessing and not curse. Jesus the disturber is our friend.

5

Heeding the Cry

There was much talk of voter apathy in the 1972 presidential election campaign. Indeed, apathy is all too characteristic of the mood of the '70s. Undoubtedly this apathy will not prove to be permanent. New issues and new causes will rouse us again. Yet there is reason to see in the current apathy toward public events a symptom of a longer and a deeper trend.

Apathy is a bad word in our vocabulary. We forget that it was once used by some of our Greek forebears, especially the Stoics, to describe the ideal state or condition of man. To be free from concern about what happens outside one's sphere of control was, for the Stoic, salvation. That meant that the Stoic strove mightily to become virtuous in himself while cultivating indifference toward external occurrences.

We are heirs of the alternative view that emotional involvement in public events and concern about them are essential to our humanity. But that view arose with the Hebrew prophets who saw Yahweh as stern moral will and omnipotent Lord of history. This is a vision which, for good or ill, we do not share. It was sustained by a story of his mighty acts that no longer fits our apprehension of nature or history. It climaxed in an expectation of final judgment that cannot be identified with our fears of an end brought about by atomic war or environmental collapse.

If history has no Lord, and if we individually do not stand under the moral judgment of a transcendent maker, then does our continued concern for critical openness and historical responsibility make sense? Why worry how we write a chapter in a book that has no end, or at least no end that makes sense of the story leading to it? On the way to universal extinction, why take ourselves so seriously?

When we face these questions we can take some comfort in the great humanists of our century who, without belief in the prophetic God, continued the prophetic witness. Bertrand Russell is one such humanist. Few professing Christians have matched his record of responsible and costly involvement in the events of this century. By word and deed he has quickened the conscience of us all.

But on closer inspection Russell is not so hopeful an example as he seems. We are not asking whether there are heroic prophets who continue the witness to truth and righteousness in our time. We are asking instead whether there is any reason to continue this style of existence when its original grounds are lacking. In answering that question, we find that Russell is of little help. Reflecting on his own intense opposition to Nazism, Russell sought its grounds. Finally, he decided, it must be admitted to be merely a matter of taste.

Russell seems to be in much the same position as many of us liberal Christians. We are living off inherited capital. Those things we care most about seem not to be grounded in our present convictions about reality. We speak of what we "still" believe. We sense that crucial beliefs are slipping from us. We have no will to impose such beliefs on our children, and if we did, we would have no way. With the passing of prophetic theism, prophetic humanism fades too.

There is little mystery about where present religious trends are leading. When men cease to live in terms of meaningful history, they will inevitably revert to more ancient sources of meaning. Perhaps the historical consciousness has never been more than a thin overlay over the mystical and archaic one for most men. Perhaps the image of return describes the deepest longing of the human heart.

Theodore Roszak showed himself to be a brilliant critic of our dominant technological society in *The Making of a Counter-Culture*. More recently, he has published a book entitled *Where the Wasteland Ends: Politics and Transcendence in Postindustrial Society*. In it, he is calling for the reaffirmation of God in order to rally the forces of the spirit against the dehumanizing society and mentality that oppress us. But the God he affirms is not the prophetic-Christian one; it is, rather, the archaic one. He condemns Christianity for having opposed such esoteric cults as magic and alchemy. Only through a revival of these mysteries, in his view, can we break out of the bondage to the rational through which we are bound to our repressive society as well.

The personal faith of Richard Rubenstein exemplifies this return to the archaic in a peculiarly lucid way:

"The biblical Lord of history is a redeemer God. He promises that the sorrows of the present age will ultimately be vindicated by the triumph of his kingdom. This view implies that human history has a meaning and a goal—the coming of God's kingdom. Unfortunately, nothing in our anthropological, biological, or psychological knowledge of man offers the slightest justification for his belief. . . . Man is the most cunning and predatory of all animals. He hardly seems a fit candidate for citizenship in the divine commonwealth. The Judaeo-Christian belief in the redeemer God is in reality the collective dream of Western man. . . .

". . . There is a conception of God which does not falsify reality and which remains meaningful after the death of the God-who-acts-in-history. It is in fact a very old conception of God with deep roots in both Western and Oriental mysticism. According to this conception, God is spoken of as the Holy Nothingness. . . . He is an indivisible *plenum* so rich that all existence derives from his very essence. . . .

"Perhaps the best available metaphor for the conception of God as the Holy Nothingness is that God is the ocean and we are the waves. In some sense each wave has its moment in which it is distinguishable as a somewhat separate entity. Nevertheless, no wave is entirely distinct from the ocean which is its substantial ground. The waves are surface manifestations of the ocean." (Richard Rubenstein, *Morality and Eros,* pp. 185–186; Mc-Graw-Hill Book Co., Inc., 1970.)

It seems that when we deny the Father God as the transcendent creator, lord and judge of history, we find ourselves drawn back to the Mother Goddess who is the undifferentiated totality from which we are distinguished only provisionally and temporarily. She offers us release from all tension, reunion with the One, return to the beginning. But in the absence of hope for a better future, history is meaningless. In the absence of judgment, ethics returns to the social mores from which it arose. In the absence of real individuality, the person loses significance.

What, then, about us? We are drawn by the currents of our time toward this archaic vision. We cannot affirm the traditional transcendent prophetic God. Yet we believe in the importance of history, we live out of some kind of hope, our individuality seems to us real and valuable, and the prophetic passion for justice burns within us. Must we say of all this that it is "still" true, that is, that it is vestigial and doomed to pass away? Or is there an alternative to the Father God of the prophets and the Mother Goddess of the archaic and mystical visions?

There is an alternative, one deeply rooted in our Christian tradition, repeatedly affirmed in the recent past, yet still awaiting a formulation that can effectively grasp and shape the imagination. It is the vision of the incarnate God.

Thomas Altizer has struggled for an adequate formulation of this vision. He had taken as his starting point the kenotic hymn in Phil. 2:5–11. This speaks of Christ as emptying himself to assume human form. For Altizer, this means that the transcendent gives itself up to immanence, that spirit becomes flesh, that is, that God becomes man. Christ is the name for the ensuing movement of the divine within the world.

In this way Altizer affirms the forward movement of history.

We are called, not to return to the primordial, but to go forward with Christ to the End.

Altizer points the way for us, but to follow him altogether would be to betray the convictions whose grounding we seek. Altizer insists that the End to which Christ leads differs from the primordial ground. But he is not able to make this difference clear. Like the exponents of archaic religion, he uses images of a Totality that is beyond differentiation. For him, too, ethical, social, and political concerns are displaced from importance in the Christian vision.

Is there a way of understanding the incarnate God that does meet our need? To put the question so baldly is to suggest that we are trying to construct a God to fulfill our wishes rather than openly seeking to know reality as it is. But that is not quite the case. We begin with our commitment to the open and critical spirit, our concern for ourselves as human beings and for our neighbors, our longing for justice in human affairs, and our desire to participate responsibly in history, and we ask, Are all these quite unfounded? Is our concern for these things simply a matter of taste or the product of a wish-fulfilling dream? And the affirmative answer to that question does not ring true. It is hard to believe that these concerns are simply arbitrary or fashioned to fulfill our needs, when they are in tension with the more obvious desires rooted in our organisms. Certainly these concerns are the product of some process that has been working its way through the histories that have fashioned us, and certainly there have been ideas associated with those histories that we can no longer believe. But what of the process itself? Is it simply the function of error? Or can it be that the process that has aroused these concerns in us has its own reality, that our continued sense of the importance of these concerns even when the beliefs that once grounded them have gone is fostered by the continuing functioning of that process, that this process has still more work to do in the world, that it is worthy of our attention and cooperation?

If there is such a process, we should be able to discern it elsewhere as well. And, in fact, we are much inclined to do so. We
see it in the hopefulness and zest of children, in the tenderness
of lovers, in the courage and zeal of revolutionaries, in the creativity of artists, in the awakening of a mind to truth, in the sensitivity of an effective counselor, in an athlete's quest of excellence, in the longing for peace with justice for all men. And
there are special moments in history to which we turn. There is
Socrates drinking the hemlock rather than employ persuasive
tricks in place of objective rational argument. There is Gautama
receiving enlightenment under the Indian tree and teaching his
disciples the way of moderation and compassion. There is Jesus
dying on a cross.

We experience a deep unity in all of these. They manifest to
us what is most precious and worthy. We feel that it is right and
good, not that we should imitate these men, but that we should
be responsive as they were responsive. That means that consciously or unconsciously we do discern in this process a direction and a character that we trust, with which we want to be in
tune and which it seems appropriate to celebrate.

If we try to specify more exactly what it is that unites these
many events and persons, we may best say that it is a movement
of transcendence. I do not mean by transcendence something
that is outside the events. I mean, rather, a movement within
the events beyond what is given by the settled situation toward
a wider and a richer future. We must picture these events not
as driven by the past but as drawn by and into the creative possibilities of the future. In our own continuing experience we can
discern that alongside the many forces that lead us to repetitive
and empty gestures, to defense of ourselves against the risk of
pain, to managing and distancing others so that they will not
break into our security, there is another voice that calls us to
openness to the other, to exposure of our settled beliefs to novel
facts and ideas, to following new and promising roads even when
we cannot know where they will lead, to the free acceptance of

responsibility for movements whose ends are wider than our own self-interest. Nikos Kazantzakis, the Greek poet and novelist, once put it this way:

"Blowing through heaven and earth, and in our hearts and the heart of every living thing, is a gigantic breath—a great Cry—which we call God. Plant life wished to continue its motionless sleep next to stagnant waters, but the Cry leaped up within it and violently shook its roots: 'Away, let go of the earth, walk!' Had the tree been able to think and judge, it would have cried, 'I don't want to. What are you urging me to do! You are demanding the impossible!' But the Cry, without pity, kept shaking its roots and shouting, 'Away, let go of the earth, walk!'

"It shouted in this way for thousands of eons; and lo! as a result of desire and struggle, life escaped the motionless tree and was liberated.

"Animals appeared—worms—making themselves at home in water and mud. 'We're just fine here,' they said. 'We have peace and security; we're not budging!'

"But the terrible Cry hammered itself pitilessly into their loins. 'Leave the mud, stand up, give birth to your betters!'

" 'We don't want to! We can't!'

" 'You can't, but I can. Stand up!'

"And lo! after thousands of eons, man emerged, trembling on his still unsolid legs.

"The human being is a centaur; his equine hoofs are planted in the ground, but his body from breast to head is worked on and tormented by the merciless Cry. He has been fighting, again for thousands of eons, to draw himself, like a sword, out of his animalistic scabbard. He is also fighting—this is his new struggle—to draw himself out of his human scabbard. Man calls in despair, 'Where can I go? I have reached the pinnacle, beyond is the abyss.' And the Cry answers, 'I am beyond. Stand up!' " (Nikos Kazantzakis, *Report to Greco,* pp. 291–292; Simon & Schuster, Inc., 1965.)

Kazantzakis speaks with dramatic power of the terrifyingly insistent Cry. Alfred North Whitehead has written of "the tender elements of the world, which slowly and in quietness operate by love." (*Process and Reality,* p. 520; The Macmillan Company, 1929.) There is a great difference in mood, but what they speak of is the same. The Cry operates in quietness. Love in its persistence in the face of every rejection is a terrifying force.

This tender Cry, this terrifying Love, to which it is so much more comfortable to shut our ears and hearts, is the God whom we have been trying to heed as liberal Christians. It is not a figment of our imagination or a product of our wishes. It is there to be discerned if we will be attentive and perceptive.

This Cry grounds our concerns for truth and justice, not by assuring that our goals will be attained, but by calling us continually into the renewal of concern. To hear the Cry is to recognize in ourselves the inertia that opposes it. In this way it judges and condemns us.

But the Cry is not primarily judge. The Cry grounds our hope.

When we project past trends into the future, we are discouraged. We see that as men continue to struggle for power and unlimited wealth they must inevitably hasten the planet toward catastrophe. But when we discern the working of the Cry, the future opens up again. Past trends need not continue. The Cry works everywhere. In the most surprising quarters we find men moved to transcend their self-serving quest for power and wealth. Where we least expect it, compassion shows itself, men strive disinterestedly for excellence, a vision of peace moves tired hearts to try again. Even out of the clash of hostile forces arises unexpected good.

To respond to the Cry is to move with the deepest rhythm of the universe. It is not the only rhythm. In the short run it is not the most obvious. There is no guarantee of its success. It may not even save humanity from total ruin. All the same, the Cry remains the deepest rhythm. In attunement with that rhythm there can be peace in the midst of confusion and joy in the midst of suffering. There is wholeness and authenticity.

6

Renewing the Vision

What we attend to determines to a great extent how we think, feel, and act. It shapes our vision of reality. Worship is one very important means of influencing what we attend to. It makes a lot of difference whether and what we worship.

The world as it is, or reality as such, is far too complex for us to attend to it in general. Attention is always selective—extremely so. Pick up any university catalog and note the great variety of courses and how they are organized into departments. Every course deals with some aspect of reality. The aspect is selective in at least two ways. Some slice of the things that make up the world is selected for attention. And those things are looked at from a particular point of view or in terms of a particular method. For example, in a course on marine biology we would expect to deal with one segment of the living things on the planet. We would also expect to study them in terms of the categories of the biologist rather than those of the physicist or the poet. In addition, the particular perspective of the professor would be a further selective factor.

In the field of politics, so important to all of us, the selection for attention is still more extreme. The successful politician is the one who can direct attention to what is going on in such a way as to place himself in a favorable light and his opponent in an unfavorable one.

In the 1972 presidential election campaign, the Republicans were successful in drawing attention to shifts in emphasis on the part of the Democratic candidate George McGovern, his sympathy for causes such as busing for integration, amnesty, and liberalization of laws against abortion and marijuana that are farther left than most of the American people, and the danger of temporary economic dislocations caused by cutbacks in military spending and changing patterns of taxation. The Democrats were largely unsuccessful in directing attention to the close ties between Richard Nixon and the centers of economic power, the advantages to most citizens of redistribution of wealth and a shift from military to civilian spending, and such sordid tactics as those involved in the "Watergate affair."

To be effective this process of attention-directing has to point us to something that exists. Total lies usually fail. But that is small comfort. For in all the infinite complexity of reality almost anything can be found.

Consider the way in which the Nazis reshaped the German mind in the '30s. Certainly they told some outright lies, but they won political power by directing attention to selected features of reality. These were lifted out of context, exaggerated, and distorted, but they were there.

There *was* injustice in the Versailles treaty, the presence of a Jewish community within an otherwise homogeneous culture *did* cause frictions, some Jews *had* been quite successful in business, and the Aryan race *did* have much to be proud of in its history and culture. By constantly calling attention to these features of reality and by constantly obscuring other, more important, features, the Nazis brought into being a quite new pattern of perception and understanding, a quite new vision of reality, that could be used to justify the most hideous acts.

Worship is the major way in which the church through the centuries has directed attention to those aspects of reality which it has thought most important. Although some of the prophets, such as Amos, denounced the worship of their day, the truth of the prophets has been made effective in history chiefly as attention has been directed to it in and through worship.

Not all acts of attention-directing are worship. The study of marine biology is not worship. The Republican and the Democratic political campaigns are not acts of worship, although there are liturgical elements within them. Even the great rallies at which the Nazis shaped the minds and destinies of hundreds of thousands of Germans were not quite worship, although they came very close.

These political movements direct attention to historical events understood to have temporary importance for some segment of mankind. Worship directs attention to what is felt as more encompassing, more basic, more ultimate, although it uses the more immediate as a means and points to it as an expression.

Some services of worship include a period for the sharing of concerns. This sharing of concerns is not in itself worship. The concerns may focus on the needs of the aged or on the protest against the war. As such, the statements of concern are social and political. But they are appropriate insofar as they give concreteness to ultimate commitments. The instances can function as part of worship insofar as they help to direct attention to the common and fundamental convictions that ground concern in individual cases.

One of the great problems of the church in every age is to find the right relation between the general and the particular or the ultimate and the relative. If worship calls attention only to that which is most basic and inclusive, many Christians will fail to grasp either the meaning or the implications of what they see. If worship directs attention primarily to the specific meaning of faith in particular circumstances, the ultimate will be falsely identified with instances. Also, judgments and theories on which Christians may legitimately differ inevitably enter into the selection of the instances.

This is a tension with which the church must always live. It becomes peculiarly acute in a time like ours when the ultimate as the Christian knows it is so hard to discern.

For worship to be effective, as is true for any means of directing attention, it must direct us to something we perceive as real and important when it is attended to. Too often in church services today what is said and done is felt by many of the most perceptive participants to belong to an unreal world. When this is the case, the participant, in defense of his integrity, must refuse the proffered vision. Then, of course, worship fails.

But when, in order to avoid this unreality, worship is brought into close relation with ordinary experience, then there is danger that it will lose its Christian substance. For worship to be Christian, attention must be directed toward something that is not simply identical with what is looked at most of the time. There must be some tension between the vision embodied in worship and the ordinary perception of reality.

I can make this point better with an example. Shortly before the Olympics were to be held in Tokyo, I was visited in Claremont by two Shinto priests. They were part of a committee to plan the use of flags for the Olympics. This provided them with an excuse for a tour of the world. They were using this opportunity to talk with representatives of other religions.

In the course of the conversation I spoke of how Christians in different countries tended to support their several governments in taking up arms against each other. More generally I was confessing the failure of Christianity to prevent its identification with national cultures.

I was somewhat taken aback, although I should not have been, when the priests asked, quite innocently, what was wrong with that? Was that not the proper function of religion? It was their view that their task as Shinto priests was to express, celebrate, and strengthen the spirit of Japan.

Christian worship all too often tends in that direction. It is hard for any of us to distinguish the values of our national culture, or of some subculture within it, from ultimate values. But most Christians would nevertheless react, as I did, with some surprise to the suggestion that no distinction is desirable. The relation is, for us at least, a problem.

Is it possible for worship to be at once real and Christian? The answer to that question may not be the same for all of us. Hence I shall state quite personally how, for me, worship both points to what I acknowledge to be real and remains in tension with my ordinary perceptions as these are shaped by my general experience.

I know that I am not the center of the universe, but I continually relapse into feeling and thinking as if I were. That relapse is checked in a variety of ways, but most of my general experience strengthens it rather than checks it. Worship, on the other hand, directs my attention to my finitude. It renews my conviction that I am only one among many, and it shapes my feelings and motives in a way that is more appropriate to that fact.

My tendency much of the time is to become settled in my attitudes and opinions. In the course of an ordinary week I defend them and extend them. They tend to become increasingly fixed bases for the evaluation of new ideas. I become less open to points of view that are really new. In worship, on the other hand, I am reminded that reality and truth lie far beyond me and that the opinions of others deserve respectful attention. I am challenged to give up my grip on the truths I think I know for the sake of receiving the truth that makes me free.

My tendency much of the time is to attend to what is disappointing, to note the little injustices of life, to become resentful that I cannot have all the advantages, appreciation, or admiration that I suppose someone else receives. That is, my natural self-centeredness leads to dissatisfaction with my lot and a vague resentment that life has not done better by me. In worship, on the other hand, my attention is drawn to what makes life good and to the generosity with which these gifts have been bestowed on me. I become ashamed of my resentment, and a sense of gratitude is renewed.

My tendency much of the time is to become complacent about

my own goodness. I compare myself favorably with other people. But at the same time I suffer from guilt, I condemn myself for certain blunders I have committed, for failures to use important opportunities, for aspects of my personality which I seem unable to alter. Surprisingly my feelings of guilt don't make me any less critical of others. On the contrary, I am likely to try to assuage my guilt by noting how others are even worse than I and even by blaming others for my own shortcomings.

In worship this structure of misery is challenged and in some fragmentary way overcome. I am turned from comparing myself with others to comparing myself with what I may and should become. My failure stands out more starkly, my excuses are exposed, my tendency to blame others appears as the final heightening of the guilt. But at the moment of recognition of guilt, I realize that it's all right. There is no need to pretend to virtue or to defend myself, because I am already pardoned. I can turn away from guilt and begin again freely to deal with the new opportunities of the new day.

My tendency much of the time is to give up on the public issues of our time. I see an urgency of change in one direction for our very survival, and I see a continuing movement in a quite different direction. I see the church which might provide the spiritual dynamic for a great repentance profoundly unsure of itself and able to do little more than seek its own survival.

In worship I am brought face to face again with the mystery that checks my gloom and defeatism. My attention is called to a power that works for good within me and among others. I realize that my own impotence does not limit this power for good and that indeed when I attend to that power I am not so wholly impotent after all. Even I can be a participant in its work. I do not have to know the outcome in order to experience hope.

In worship, then, I am renewed by attending to that which is central to all reality, that which gives, judges, and forgives, and that which works for good and grounds hope. That, of course, is God.

I have been speaking of real potentialities of quite ordinary

Christian worship. But rarely are all of them realized in a single service. Sometimes I seem to be hardly touched at all by what takes place, and I find it all too easy to understand why so many have dropped out of worship altogether. To make these potentialities real is an important responsibility for all who share in the shaping of services of worship. But even if the potentialities of traditional worship were fully realized, that would not be enough. Today we need to attend to aspects of reality that traditional worship has screened out.

For one thng, most traditional worship tends to estrange us from our bodies and our sexuality. The discomfort and confusion experienced about sexuality in most Christian cultures is intensified by worship. In reaction against those pagan cults in which sex and the divine were too nearly identified, our tradition has separated them far too much. Our worship has tended to desexualize us. We can rejoice to see the return of the dance and the physical embrace to our services, but that alone does not suffice.

Another need, urgent in our time, is the overcoming of our Christian exclusiveness. Our worship has traditionally strengthened our experience of our Christian corporateness—and that is good. But it has tended to do so in such a way as to set ourselves apart from other traditions and communities. We need to learn how to attend to those aspects of reality highlighted in other traditions without losing sight of those which have been stressed in ours.

Traditional worship focuses on our relation to God and to our neighbors in such a way as to obscure our kinship with animal and plant life. It leads us to think of ourselves as actors on the stage of nature rather than as participants in the natural process. Here we can learn much from other traditions, but we cannot simply appropriate them. We must learn this as a new lesson in our own context of beliefs and understanding of man.

Finally, our traditional worship centers on the word. The word is the central means of directing attention. In the writing of this chapter, I have been using words, too many of them perhaps, to direct attention to the importance of how we direct attention. The primary task of worship is to direct attention more effectively and more healingly. But we are learning that there is another response to the recognition that all experience is selective. There are techniques developed especially by Hindus and Buddhists for achieving a state of consciousness that is not selective, or that is at least much less selective. That consciousness is expressed in silence rather than in words. We are now challenged to incorporate such meditative silence into our worship without abandoning the Word.

Often we leave our services of worship, especially we liberal Protestants, with a renewed sense of the problems of the world, the needs to be met, the work to be done. I am suggesting that in the area of worship there is work to be done.

But the final note of worship cannot be exhortation. You and I will not save the world. We will not even transform the worship of liberal Christians. Our contributions, even if we make them, will be slight. If we are to make even those slight contributions, we individually and collectively need to be reassured precisely that everything does *not* depend on us. We need our attention directed toward the tasks to which we are called, but still more we need our attention directed to that which uses for good even our failure to fulfill our task. We don't have to succeed, because the last word of preaching, the last word of worship, the last word of the gospel, the last word of reality is grace.

7

Gratitude for Life

Grace is the final word of worship and the underlying experience of Christian life. But "grace" as a word has become foreign to our ordinary language. It appears now only as part of a technical sacred language that is little related to daily living. This chapter and the two that follow, on gratitude, trust, and justification, are attempts to make real for our situation aspects of the historic meaning of grace.

Luke tells a story of Jesus meeting ten lepers (Luke 17:11–18). In response to their cry for help he sends them to show themselves to the priests. All are cured of the dread disease, but only one returns to thank Jesus.

How much one has to be grateful for doesn't have much to do with how grateful he is. Luke drove home that point in this story. It was driven home to me again on a tourist trip to Coconut Island, not far from Honolulu. For several minutes the captain told us about the former owner, Chris Holmes, in terms calculated to arouse our envy. Holmes apparently had everything a man could want. He was able to turn his beautiful tropical island into a miniature paradise exactly according to his desires. But at the height of his fortune, he killed himself.

It is ironic that some people who have so much despair of life and destroy it, whereas others who have so little cling to it.

Those who are objectively the most fortunate sometimes are the most miserable, whereas others who have suffered terribly in outward ways are thankful for the gift of life.

Whether a man is grateful for what comes to him or resentful for what he lacks depends upon his basic orientation in life. Luke suggests that grateful men are in a small minority. Most people compare their lots with those of others who are in many respects like them, but who in some particular seem more fortunate. However well off they become financially, for example, there is always someone else who, by luck, has come out ahead. There is always some benefit of wealth that still lies beyond their means.

If a man's interest is directed not so much to material possessions as to sexual enjoyment, he will compare himself with someone else who seems more fortunate. Even if he enjoys a full and healthy sex life, he can find someone else who is more attractive to the opposite sex and more able to enjoy his conquests. There is always some real or imagined pleasure that is still denied him.

In the academic profession each person tends to look at the colleague who is a step ahead. If one lacks a position, he compares himself with another person who has secured one. If one has trouble attracting students to his classes, he compares himself with a more popular teacher. If one has not published a book, he compares himself with a colleague who has. If one has published a book, he compares himself with an author whose book has been more widely or more favorably discussed.

This tendency to compare ourselves with those who seem a little better off is basic to our competitive system. It goads us to greater efforts that are often socially constructive.

But looking at ourselves in comparison with those who are a step ahead is not calculated to make us happy. Instead, it breeds restlessness and anxiety. Further, ungrudging admiration for someone who is a little more fortunate is very rare. We have a strong tendency to think that his success is not due to any real merit on his part. We suppose that the one who has the job we lack had connections or pulled strings; that the one who is more popular uses questionable devices; that the one who published first shirked his other duties in order to do so; and so forth. Thus comparison with those who are more fortunate than ourselves breeds envy and resentment. Since there is always someone who is a step ahead, or seems to be so, and since there is always some good that we lack, no amount of success in our chosen direction brings us the happiness we expect. Looking at life in this way, we see no cause for gratitude.

One might advise that instead of comparing ourselves with others who have, or seem to have, more, we should compare ourselves with those who are less fortunate. Indeed, that advice is frequently offered. Just before we stuff ourselves on Thanksgiving turkey, we are reminded that we should remember the starving.

We should indeed be mindful of those who are less fortunate, but that has its own dangers. If we compare ourselves with those who are much worse off, we are likely to feel pity rather than gratitude. Pity tends to be a complacent and ineffective feeling that rarely leads to action. We pity the hungry while we eat our turkey. We feel rather complacent about ourselves. We may express thanks that we are not in the situation of those other miserable wretches, but our thanks are smug and self-congratulatory.

If we compare ourselves instead with those who are just below us, our competitors for the social rewards we both desire, then we feel threatened. We resent the resentment of those we have worsted. We think we deserve their respect and we receive their envy instead. We are driven to work harder to maintain our advantage over them. In this competition there is no secure resting place. Gratitude has no place in our feelings.

The problems that arise from the competitive quest for the goods of life have been recognized for thousands of years. One response has been to cut the nerve of desire that underlies all these comparisons and the resulting unhappiness. If man can never succeed in achieving what he desires, is it not better to cease desiring it?

That view has been taken very seriously and consistently by Buddhists and Stoics. They show that by desiring nothing at all or only those goods which are within our own power to realize, we can be free from the endless unhappiness of comparing ourselves enviously and defensively with others.

Many others have agreed that to set one's heart on wealth, sexual fulfillment, and professional success is a mistake. They hold that when we orient our lives around goals of this sort, we condemn ourselves to disappointment. They teach that only spiritual values are really worth attaining, and that if we sincerely seek these, we will receive them.

There is a profound wisdom in these doctrines, and people have achieved a good deal of serenity by practicing them. Much of our unhappiness does stem from setting our hearts on the wrong things. Especially the competitive element in these desires is wrong. These worldly goods should be subordinated to personal relations, justice for all, and ultimately the vision of God.

But Christianity cannot share in belittling the value of wealth, sex, and success. Christians think of the world as creation. Even in its crassest physical expressions, the world is good. God desires its existence and fulfills his purposes through it. The Christian cannot be indifferent to worldly goods. He is instead grateful for them.

Christian gratitude is not based upon comparison with others. To be grateful for being richer, sexier, or more successful than another is arrogance and selfishness. True gratitude can arise only when we give up comparisons and view life in an "absolute" way.

"Absolute" is a tricky word. It suggests something very mysterious, whereas what is intended here is fairly simple. By viewing things absolutely I mean seeing them just as they are in themselves. Most of the time it seems that to think of something as good is to think of it as better than something else. We are inveterate comparers. But it is also possible to ask whether it is good in itself. If we must compare, we can ask whether it is better than nothing at all. That helps us to answer the question.

But the question of whether something is good need not involve any comparison at all.

If I am hungry and I am given a bowl of vegetable soup, I can appreciate that soup as good. I am not pronouncing it to be better or worse than something else I might have received, such as clam chowder. I am simply judging it as it is.

When we press down to the most fundamental level of our attitude, we come to absolute judgments of some kind. They are usually not conscious, but they govern consciousness. The comparative judgments that we consciously make are determined by them.

One unconscious, absolute judgment that many people make about life is that it is a task. They find themselves driven to achieve something. The meaning of life is measured by its success in attaining set goals. Comparisons with others follow along the lines set by these goals. Life as a whole is a strenuous effort. Some satisfaction can be taken in partial success, but for the most part life cheats a person of the fruits of his effort. Time erodes achievements. The most that can be done is to pass on the torch to others. The ultimate image of this experience of life is that of Sisyphus through all eternity pushing his stone up to the top of a mountain only to have it roll down again.

Others have been disillusioned by the consequences of the view of life as a task. If the goals cannot be reached, or if they are worthless in themselves, then the whole thing is ridiculous, absurd. Man is thrown into a swirl of events that do not add up or go anywhere. Everything is chance and necessity without meaning or purpose.

At this fundamental level of interpretation argument is out of place. There is no disproof of the view of life as "thrownness." But the philosopher whose analysis of human existence gave clearest expression to this way of understanding—Martin Heidegger—went on himself to another perception, one in which thankfulness dominated.

Rather than noticing the arbitrariness of our place in a meaningless world, we may experience life, the sheer fact of being alive, as good. We see that life is given to us freely in every moment as a fresh opportunity to be and to do and to enjoy. The means of preserving life are generally pleasant as well as necessary. And for most of us life makes possible more sophisticated pleasures as well. We have cause to be grateful.

This Christian understanding of man's situation leads to the affirmation of life as it is given. It closely resembles the spirit of other traditions, such as that expressed in this beautiful poem from Zen Buddhism:

> In spring, the flowers, and in autumn the moon,
> In summer a refreshing breeze, and in winter the snow.
> What else do I have need of?
> Each hour to me is an hour of joy.

(Quoted from Edward Conze, *Buddhism: Its Essence and Development*, p. 205; Harper & Row, Publishers, Inc., Harper Torchbook, 1959.)

Surely the spirit of sheer immediacy in this poem is very close to the spirit of gratitude as the Christian knows it. The enlightened Buddhist in the Zen tradition accepts what comes in its immediate goodness. He does not compare what he experiences with anything else. He wastes no time on regrets or on envy of others. He is aware of what is as it is, and he affirms it. He does not inquire into the future consequences of events. The simple and direct awareness of what is present to him drives out all anxiety and restlessness.

Yet just here, where the spirit of Buddhism is so close to that of Christianity, differences appear. The Christian too is called to enjoy the flowers, the moon, the breeze, and the snow. But he is called to respond in gratitude. Since he has received such gifts, it is his opportunity and task to share with others. To whom much is given, from him much is expected. The Israelite knew himself to be especially blessed by God. For that reason, in gratitude for God's gifts, he was called to costly service.

One reason that the spirit of gratitude has become so rare in our culture is that it has been mistaken for its perverted forms. Against these we have rightly reacted in disgust.

Pollyanna symbolizes one of these perversions. The logic of this perversion is superficially sound. The Christian sees life as good. He does not compare what comes to him with what comes to others. Must he not then deny the reality of evil and give up all realistic appraisal?

The answer is no. Pain and anxiety and separation and cruelty are part of what comes to each of us, and they are evil. In some cases they may contribute to a later and a larger good, but there is no guarantee of that. To believe that, in spite of this evil, life remains fundamentally good prevents us from being preoccupied with evil and from growing resentful and envious, but it does not hinder recognition of evil for what it is. On the contrary, it is only in the context of appreciation of the goodness of life that evil is fully recognized. Evil is the destruction of life. The more we love life and are grateful for the gift of life, the more sensitive we are to the ways in which life is curtailed and distorted.

The emphasis that life should be viewed absolutely rather than comparatively leads all too readily to a second perversion. Without comparing the conditions of men and our own condition with that of others, we cannot attend to questions of justice.

To guard against that perversion we must make a clear distinction between our most fundamental stance toward reality and the secondary activities that are allowed and encouraged within it. The basic Christian stance is one of thankfulness. But thankfulness is appreciation for real goods. How goods are distributed is important in a world in which what happens matters.

When we are victims of injustice, we do well to recognize that fact both for our own sakes and for others' sakes as well. Even more important, we must never allow our appreciation for the goodness of all life to dull our awareness of the injustices inflicted upon others. It has done so at times in Christendom. It was in a Christian culture that Karl Marx called religion the opiate of the people. But the prophetic spirit that is our Jewish heritage, the spirit embodied also in Marx, reminds us repeatedly that the grateful man is active in behalf of the oppressed.

There is a third perversion, more dangerous perhaps, because so close to the true spirit of gratitude. It is symbolized in the flower children of a few years ago.

Central to the lesson that many young people tried to teach us in the '60s is the idea that life is to be enjoyed. They saw that their parents too often treated life as a task, a heavy burden, a labor to be accomplished. The youth protested that in working always for future happiness, we have ignored the goodness of what is already at hand. We have built a society that prizes expensive and difficult goods accessible only through the accumulation of wealth. Advertising suggests to us that we can be happy only by traveling to distant places, having fine food and clothing, owning luxurious homes, automobiles, and motorboats. We neglect the simple and readily accessible goods—the beauty of nature, the enjoyment of friends and family, even the taste of simple foods.

This lesson has been needed. Young people taught us dramatically by public flouting of false, conventional values. They rejected competition in favor of those values which we can all enjoy together. By returning to simpler and more natural lifestyles, some of them have shown that we do not have to submit ourselves so painfully to the pressures of earning a living.

But the lesson has been simplistic and one-sided. Not all effort is misdirected. Not all of the complexity of life is artificial and false. The richest values are not always the simplest ones. There are goals worth working for, and there is value in the process of seeking as well as in what is found. To affirm that life is good and to be grateful for it need not be to turn our backs on the achievements of civilization. These, too, are embodiments of life. If life is good, its refinement and its manifold expressions are also good.

To have the spirit of gratitude, then, is to affirm what comes. We are to enjoy it, but not without responsibility. We are to affirm the fundamental goodness of life but not so as to acquiesce in the power of evil as it thwarts and destroys life. We are to rejoice in life as it comes to each of us individually, but to remain concerned for justice in the distribution of what is valuable. We are to savor the elemental in life, but not in such a way as to disparage the more complex expressions of life in art and science.

When we understand what the spirit of gratitude is, we may decide that we ought to be thankful. Or when we see that the grateful man enjoys life in a way which is closed to others, we may desire to become more appreciative. In either case, we will seek ways and means of changing our attitude. And to some extent that is possible. As children we sang, "Count your many blessings, name them one by one." And it is true that thinking about our blessings does more to make us grateful toward life than does nursing our grievances. As adults we have been told by Norman Vincent Peale about "the power of positive thinking," and there is no doubt that some have found improvement through practicing the techniques he recommends.

However, these are superficial approaches to the problem. They alter temporarily our conscious attitudes, sometimes masking deep resentments underneath. By concealing from us the negativism of our fundamental attitudes, they can hinder the change that is really needed.

What is needed is to experience all life as grace. That means to experience it as a gift and to experience the gift as good. Grace means unearned favor. Life is not thrust upon us but is offered to us as opportunity. We have done nothing to merit this gift. It is completely free. And with all its problems and ambiguities it remains fundamentally and absolutely good.

The word "grace" has faded from our vocabulary. The experience of life as a free gift has declined. These two occurrences are both cause and effect of each other. Our sense of the burdensomeness of life and our resentment toward it have crowded out the experience of grace. With the loss of the word the moments in which life is known in its goodness and givenness pass by unnamed. What is unnamed is little noticed. What is little noticed fades from effectiveness. If the goodness and freeness of life are to be recognized again, the word "grace" must be restored to power. Where life is known as grace, gratitude springs naturally from the heart.

But how can this change occur? How can we cease to see life as pressure, demand, and pain and view it instead as grace? If we do not experience life as grace, it does not help to pretend that we do. It is much better to express frankly our disappointment with life than to feel a resentment we conceal even from ourselves. Sometimes it happens that by working through our negative feelings we become open for affirmative ones. We must trust the truth.

We can trust the truth, because life *is* grace. It is given to us, and what is given is good. That is the gospel, and it can renew itself in all its strangeness to the modern ear. When we hear it, then from time to time what it announces rings true. In those moments, whether things are going well for us or badly, gratitude becomes a reality. Gratitude, too, is a gift.

8

Trusting and Deciding

The words "trust" and "decision" point to two quite different styles of life. "Trust" suggests that we let others make the choices for us. "Decision" suggests that we take the responsibility upon ourselves.

Both words have an important place in describing the Christian life. On the one hand, there is the slogan for trusting: "Let go, and let God." On the other hand, there is the slogan for responsible decision-making: "God has no hands but our hands."

These two themes are in obvious tension. One points to an emptying of oneself and passivity. We used to sing: "He is the potter, we are the clay." But we also sang "Onward, Christian Soldiers" and talked of building the Kingdom of God.

Is Christianity simply self-contradictory in affirming both of these? Should we choose one against the other? If so, which?

In the '70s our wise men and teachers are encouraging trust. As individuals we are urged to recognize our need for help. We have been trying to solve our problems by reason and will, and we have failed. We have tried to control our feelings and make both our feelings and our actions conform to principles in which we rationally believe. The result has been a stifling of feeling and a failure of action. We need to develop an attitude of trust toward others and toward the unconscious levels of our own being.

In small groups we have been learning again to trust one another. We have risked sharing our feelings and found that they were accepted. Others appreciate our openness. We thought they would despise us because of our weakness, and we find that instead they love us when they know us as we really are. It is an exhilarating experience.

Even more difficult for many of us than trusting one another is to trust the deeper dimensions of our own individual being. I speak here from painful experience of failure to trust my own unconscious and my body.

One of my vivid, and vividly unpleasant, memories of childhood is of piano recitals. Anticipation of such recitals clouded many weeks of my life. As the day came closer I would be gripped by anxiety. I would practice, and I would have no problem playing the piece by heart at home. But I was terrified that when playing before others I would forget. And of course such expectation is self-fulfilling. Sometimes I did forget. I remember one time especially. It was a piece in which the first part was repeated once before the end was played. I got through that far, but then I could not think how to make the transition to the last part of the piece. The knowledge was, of course, well established in my fingers and muscles. But I could not trust my body. I was reduced to playing the first portion a third time and then retiring in humiliation.

My case was an extreme one. Many people are able to develop great skills and to trust their bodies to perform well. But we are learning today that we have trusted our bodies far too little. Our culture has turned our bodies into instruments for the effecting of rational purposes. We have strengthened our wills precisely by denying our bodies the satisfaction of their needs. Even among primitive peoples men established their manhood by forcing their bodies to perform unnatural feats of suffering and endurance at the behest of their minds. We have now learned that the whole history of civilization has involved suppression of the body and its natural rhythms, needs, and wisdom.

When men cease to control and manipulate their bodies and

the feelings that are most closely related to them, they enter into a quite different experience. The tension goes out of them. They have a new wholeness and spontaneity. Their imagination floats free. They become more creative. In these and other ways the attitude of trust opens us to resources for fulfilling our desires that are closed to us as long as we attempt to win our goals by controlled action.

Even so, it would be a serious mistake to take this trusting attitude uncritically. The body, the unconscious, and other persons are not wholly trustworthy. Animals have a bodily wisdom that causes them in general to eat what is good for them, but they can be tricked into eating poisoned food. The wisdom of our bodies is no greater. The attitude of trust toward others can be exploited by con artists. Madison Avenue advertising can manipulate our trust for the enrichment of business or the advantage of a politician. In the end it seems best to trust others and our bodies and unconscious only as far as critical reflection on the consequences of such trust justifies it.

This should be no news to a Christian. In traditional language it would be idolatrous to trust the body or the unconscious or other people in any unqualified way. Unqualified trust should be placed only in the One who is absolutely trustworthy, and that is God.

But practically speaking, what does it mean to trust God when we face a decision? Does it mean to go limp and see what happens? Sometimes it has meant that. In the Old Testament we read of the casting of lots in order to learn God's will. In the Middle Ages there were trials by ordeal. John Wesley used to close his eyes, open the Bible at random, and then place his finger on a verse, supposing that God would so control the movement of his hand that the verse would answer his question.

Few of us believe in these practices. Yet when God is thought of as being outside us, working on us like an external force, these customs are understandable. The idea is to remove human control from the situation on the assumption that when this is done and divine aid invoked, the external divine power will take over. In this picture the antithesis of trust and deciding remains. To trust is to give up human decision in favor of what is supposed to be divine guidance. Man reduces himself to a puppet in order that God's will may be done.

Most Christians who have understood trusting in this way have wisely preferred to assume responsibility for their own decisions. Is it not best to decide by rational evidence how far to trust what—even reputed means of letting God make the decision? Are we not condemned to depend finally upon the individual and independent will to act, and upon reason to guide the action to the right end? Instead of trusting something else or someone else, must we not rely upon our own thinking and deciding? Is not every attempt to escape from this total personal responsibility finally a cop-out? Does not ethics, after all, have the last word about human behavior?

Certainly ethical action is desirable, worthy, and admirable. Reason and rational action are essential. It is by thought that questions of justice and the general good are to be decided and action is to be guided toward their realization. There are many things that should be done to attain these ends regardless of how individuals feel about them.

But there are problems with the ethical life. To be strictly ethical is to be constantly deciding what to do in the light of all sorts of considerations. Even if the ethical man decides to be spontaneous, he has to be spontaneous "by the numbers." He acts spontaneously when, and as long as, his rational reflection leads him to judge that it is right to act spontaneously. In such spontaneity something is missing.

The ethical life is a burdensome one. It is hard to know what is right. There are so many claims upon us that seem justified that it is difficult to decide how to balance them against one another. We are always left with the sense that there is more to be done. We find ourselves driven and weighed down. Others sometimes find our dutiful and righteous actions oppressive. We do not enjoy life, and others enjoy life less when we are around.

Recognizing these problems, some of us make a point of not

being too righteous. We allow ourselves a few carefully selected vices. We filter out many of the claims upon us so that they will not trouble our consciences. In short, we seek moderation. We want to be ethical where it really matters but casual elsewhere, knowing how to have a good time.

Both those who strive for the full ethical life and those who for good reason dilute it with moderate self-indulgence are victims of the final corruption of such a style. That corruption is self-righteousness. The man who works diligently at acting righteously in all things knows that others do not do so. He cannot avoid recognizing his superiority even if, as a matter of principle, he avoids mentioning it. It is simply the case that, measured by the standards that are evident to him, he *is* more moral than those who cater to their own fancies without regard to the wider consequences of their acts. Those who moderate their virtue with self-indulgence in order to avoid this offense are often the more guilty of it. For they believe themselves to be superior, in true goodness, to those who go all the way in the ethical life as well.

There is an opposite problem that also afflicts the ethical man—the problem of despair. He recognizes that his ethical actions fail to achieve their goals. He seeks the good of others while actually often offending them. He redoubles his efforts to do what is right only to find that the harder he tries the less successful he is. He knows that much of the problem lies in his spirit or attitude which seems to others hard, brittle, and critical. So he tries to make himself gentle, flexible, and accepting. But his efforts to change his own spirit are frustrating and futile. The more sensitively he perceives what he ought to do and to be, the harder he tries to do and to be it, the more is he aware of the gulf that separates him from his goal. To avoid despair he may make himself less sensitive and engage in self-deception. The man who begins with a passion for total righteousness sometimes ends in a lie.

We seem to have arrived at a dilemma. On the one hand, trusting, in the sense of turning over decision to something or someone else, fails us. On the other hand, the life of ethical deciding does not attain the goodness toward which it strives.

Christianity has rightly understood that we can go beyond the ethical life only if there is a completely trustworthy reality. But traditional Christian teaching has been much less clear as to how the existence of such a reality solves our problem. When God is conceived of as an external, transcendent reality, he may be supposed to be fully trustworthy, but it is not at all clear that we have trustworthy access to his purposes. If we are told that we have such access through revelation, the problem is complicated but not helped. Do we have trustworthy assurance that revelation has occurred? Is there a trustworthy account of that revelation? And, if so, is there a trustworthy way in which the revelation can be interpreted in its relevance to the concrete situation I now face? In responding to such questions the church develops an elaborate system of apologetic theology and of moral rules much like those against which Jesus and Paul protested. Trust in God is transformed into acceptance of authority and obedience to established teaching.

If the reality of One who is trustworthy is to free us to go beyond the ethical life, that One must be trustworthily present in our experience. There is a Christian tradition of such presence as indwelling Christ, Holy Spirit, and inner light. This tradition has been profoundly hurt in its influence by exaggerated and distorted expressions, which have attracted widespread attention. In the second Christian century some Christians claimed to have been informed by the Holy Spirit just when and where Jesus was coming again in final judgment. Similar erroneous claims to private inspiration have recurred frequently in Christian history.

But the presence of the trustworthy need not be associated with visions and trances and claims to new revelations. More fundamentally it is experienced as an empowering, healing, directing, and enlivening power that operates within. If the reality of such a power can be believed, then an attitude of trust is justified.

Can we believe in the reality of such a power? Traditional language about it carries little weight with us outside the often artificial context of the church. But the inward quest for a trustworthy power is very much alive. There are two directions of this quest which together can help the liberal Christian to move forward.

In many of its forms the human potential movement is a quest for a trustworthy center within the psychic life. It teaches that when obstacles are removed, there appears an inner power which makes for healing, for growth, and for mutual love. Although some forms of the movement seem to call for a generalized trust, others are rightly concerned to direct trust toward that which is trustworthy, recognizing that many of the most powerful forces within us are dangerous. When the rational will releases its tight control over feelings, a lot of aggression and bitterness may pour out in all kinds of senseless ways. In themselves these are destructive, and their open expression must be carefully channeled. They are certainly not what is to be trusted and acted upon. The trust is rather that these negative feelings, this garbage, is not the deeper reality of the person, that beyond it and beneath it is something else. When one gets in touch with this something else, and trusts it, growth occurs.

What is trusted is sometimes thought of as the true self, and this is contrasted with the ego of ordinary experience. Since this ego is the rational will which is the agent of deciding, trusting is set sharply over against deciding. Insofar as the true self is able to organize experience and personality, the task of the ego is to relax its hold and passively allow this to happen.

The human potential movement has grown out of the discipline of healing. To the restoration of normality it has added as a goal a deeper fulfillment of human potentiality. But its disparagement of deciding in favor of trusting is connected with its inattention to ethical issues. Here lies its widely recognized limitation.

The second direction of the quest for the trustworthy is found within existentialism, where deciding, rather than trusting, has been stressed. In some of its forms existentialism has denied that there is any trustworthy ground for deciding at all. Deciding is seen as arbitrary. But even those, such as Jean-Paul Sartre, who seem to hold to this position, qualify it. Sartre's own life and teaching testify to a profound recognition of the importance of human freedom and deep sensitivity to how it is to be achieved.

What existentialists do oppose is every form of legalism. They deny that there is any body of external rules which binds us or that the superego as an internalization of such rules has final authority. Man's dignity and responsibility consist in his freedom beyond all rules. He can and must face the future in free choice. The experience, wisdom, and habits of the past should not finally determine him.

Situation ethics is a recent expression of this insight. Decision should be appropriate to the situation and not controlled by moral rules inherited from the past.

But what does it mean for action to be appropriate to the situation? How can one possible action be judged more appropriate than another? If this is not done by rules, it must be done more intuitively. The Sartrean might say: Act as freedom requires in the concrete situation. The Christian might say: Act as love requires. The meaning differs little. Both assume, unconsciously perhaps, that man can achieve a sensitivity to what is happening which enables him to see what is possible and needed. When we free ourselves from the blinders of habit and prejudice and the burden of moral rules, there is a deeper level of our moral being that grasps directly what is right and appropriate. In terms of this we can critically evaluate our actions.

Alfred North Whitehead pointed to this basic fact of ethical experience when he wrote that there is a universal "intuition of immediate occasions as failing or succeeding in reference to the ideal relevant to them. There is a rightness attained or missed, with more or less completeness of attainment or omission." (*Religion in the Making,* pp. 60–61; The Macmillan Company, 1927.)

The human potential movement works through the chaos of

our feelings to a deeper center that is the trustworthy source of healing and growth. Existentialism works through our bondage to rules and habits to uncover the trustworthy grasp of what is appropriate, what is freeing and loving, in concrete situations. That to which both come is grace.

I fear that this sounds very abstract. It is time to consider what it means in daily life to live by grace.

Suppose you sense that someone is hurt and needs reassurance. You experience that need as a claim upon yourself which is at the same time an opportunity and an impulse to act. You act as the occasion seems to require.

This differs from the model of the purely ethical life in that you do not distance yourself from the situation in order to sift the evidence, judge the contemplated action in terms of moral principles, or think through the probable consequences of various courses of behavior. Instead, you trust your sense of the situation and the impulse to act. You decide in terms of that trust.

Now, your act may turn out to be in error. You may have misinterpreted the other's expression, or even if your sense of his need was accurate, you may have blundered in your effort to reassure. You may have deepened his hurt and alienated him.

At this point you confront the key choice. How do you respond when you realize that your impulsive action failed? You may decide that trusting intuitions and acting on apparent opportunities is a mistake. That would mean that you would turn toward a more rational and calculating, that is, a more ethical, style of life.

But you may instead decide to trust grace. Then you would recognize your need to become more sensitive. That might mean that you would try to open yourself to the deeper levels of your own experience. You would work through your defensiveness and your tendency to project your own attitudes onto others and to try to control and manipulate them. Meanwhile you would continue to take the risk of acting on such light as you had, humbly learning from your mistakes.

You would do this in the conviction that there is within you a potency of real sensitivity and appropriate response. You would recognize that you cannot generate or control this potency. You cannot predetermine its contents by deducing them from rational formulas.

Trusting grace by no means excludes reasoning. The tendency to disparage reason on the part of both the human potential movement and some existentialists must be countered. The question is not whether to think but what to think about. If we try to decide what to think about by thinking alone, we are driven into a fruitless circle. The wise man is one who perceives what is appropriate to think about so that his thinking, which may be very abstract, complex, and subtle, becomes a part of the response to the actual situation. He uses thinking to clear away the impediments to accurate perception and sensitive response. What he perceives may be hidden to the man of less disciplined thought.

What of the relation of trusting and deciding when we live thus from grace? They can still be distinguished. Trusting our sense of what is needed can be distinguished from deciding to act upon it. But this does not do justice to our actual experience. The intuition of rightness is at the same time an impulse or a lure to the act. It can be resisted or rejected, and indeed there are powerful forces of habit and fear that oppose themselves to the impulse. That is why decision is necessary. But the decision operates within the impulse. It is made possible by the impulse. Insofar as it confirms the impulse, it is an act of trusting.

Trusting and deciding are both hard work. We experience the demand to trust and to decide as a heavy responsibility. But when we decide to trust and to make decisions in the context of trust, we realize that the grace we trust and for which we decide is at the same time the source of the trust and the decision. To live from grace is to receive by grace both trusting and deciding.

9

The Grace
That Justifies

The issue of *Newsweek* that appeared just after the landslide reelection of Richard Nixon reported that the President believes that this nation needs to reject permissiveness in favor of a new stress upon personal responsibility. His new administration is to be based upon this philosophy. In calling for this emphasis on the individual's duty, Nixon is in tune with deep and widespread feelings in the American public.

Some people will react to this with anger. It suggests to them a form of law and order that is little more than the imposition of the will of the strong upon the weak, or of the majority upon the minority. There is reason to fear that some of this will be involved. But it would be wrong to suppose that this is all that is meant, or even that this is what is more fundamentally intended.

My own reaction is one of sadness. I believe in individual responsibility. I believe that some of what is meant by permissiveness has done damage in our society. But a renewed stress upon moral responsibility taken by itself is an effort to recover what is not recoverable and what would not be worth recovering.

Our society has alternated between a tight moralistic pattern and a loose easygoing one. In theological jargon we talk about legalism and antinomianism. A legalistic system tries to help people find the good life by providing numerous rules by which to live. The rules often come out of rich experience and deep satisfaction with that experience on the part of one generation. But the following generations find them oppressive. They revolt against them. Sometimes in doing so they attack all rules. They call for pure spontaneity and the liberty to do whatever one wants or feels like doing as the true way of finding a whole and satisfying life. This is antilegalism or antinomianism.

Antinomianism, too, in the period of experiencing liberation from old rules, is deeply satisfying. But it does not satisfy for long. Outwardly it tends toward a chaos in which individuals find themselves less free than they had been under law. Inwardly it leads to meaninglessness. Some begin to find patterns of living that lead them out of chaos and meaninglessness. They offer these patterns to others. These become a new set of rules. Society adopts them. Legalism has returned. People revolt against it. Antinomianism follows.

The last century has illustrated this pattern. Victorianism means to us a rigid system of oppressive rules by which people pretended to live. Behind the facade we have learned to see resentment and lust. This unattractive culture had grown out of the evangelical revivals of the eighteenth century. In those revivals many people had found a new and richer life through personal and religious discipline. The children of the saved became respectable through the acceptance of that discipline. In Victoria's time they ruled England.

Many factors combined in the past half century to destroy the sway of Victorian legalism. The name of Freud can represent some of them. The new self-understanding that the psychologies derivative from him have released into our culture has deeply transformed it and affected all of us.

Freudianism exposed the hypocrisy and repressiveness of Victorianism. In doing so, with or without the approval of Freud himself, it challenged every system of rules. It encouraged an attitude of appreciation for what is most deeply rooted in our natures, what is libidinal and erotic. Expression replaced control as the dominant value. The sense of obligation was seen as the problem rather than the cure to man's ills. What one feels like doing, not what one thinks one ought to do, became the criterion of right action.

This antinomianism breeds a new legalism in two ways. First, insofar as it succeeds, it becomes a new set of rules itself. Many of us have been in groups in which in the name of complete spontaneity and honesty we felt pressed toward expressing quite limited aspects of what we were feeling and thinking. I have personally profited from such groups. But the requirement that I express only what I deeply feel and avoid all head-tripping is just as strict and difficult a rule as any that has been laid down in the name of moral obligation. It is enforced by social pressure in much the same way.

Secondly, there is revulsion against the extreme manifestations of this antinomianism. O. Hobart Mowrer a few years ago wrote a book bitterly attacking Freudianism for having undercut morality. He argued that psychological health depends upon clear and vigorous moral teaching and discipline. Some forms of contemporary therapy operate with contracts between the patient and the group. These contracts are commitments to take definite actions. They are enforced by group approval and disapproval. On a broader cultural scale we recognize the fresh articulation of the desire expressed by Richard Nixon to return to a society of responsible individuals.

Most Christians have tended toward legalism. Some have held to legalisms that are rigid and exacting. Others have followed the path of moderation. A few have rejected rules altogether in the name of the gospel of liberation. The alternation of legalism and antinomianism has been characteristic of Christian history.

Even so, on this point I dare to say that Christianity has the answer. It offers the alternative to both legalism and antinomianism that satisfies the legitimate concerns of both. It teaches grace and response. Even when as now its message is poorly understood, still it touches our lives and saves us from the final destructiveness of both life under law and the rejection of law.

The Christian position can be quickly summarized. It runs something like this: You don't have to be or do what you ought to be or do; therefore you are free to be or do it.

Very simple! Also quite bewildering. Some would say, silly. Isn't it self-contradictory to say that we don't have to do what we ought to do? Or else isn't it just stating the obvious fact that we sometimes don't do what we should? How could the fact that we don't have to do something make us free to do it? And if we are free to do what we ought to do, are we not equally free to do something quite different? Doesn't that give us a license to do evil?

These are perfectly good questions. They arose in the early church in response to the message of Paul. They have recurred whenever the gospel in its distinctiveness has been preached. They point to the fact that the Christian message is paradoxical in the sense of being against the grain of common sense. But perhaps at this point common sense is no adequate guide. Perhaps common sense runs back and forth between legalism and antinomianism and can find no way out. Perhaps we should be prepared to listen to surprising ideas and to be patient while they try to explain themselves.

We live in a psychological age. To explain a basic Christian teaching is for us, therefore, largely a matter of explaining it psychologically. In the process something may be lost of the original meaning, but psychology is a good place to begin.

Paul too gave a psychological account of the problem in Rom. 7:7–12. He said that as an infant he had natural and spontaneous desires which were perfectly innocent. In that condition he was very much alive. But as he grew older he learned that he ought not to desire things which belonged to other people. He recognized that and he tried to obey it. But recognizing the value of the rule did not destroy the desires that went counter to it. Instead, he found that the knowledge that he ought not to want certain things made him want them even more. The harder he tried to obey the law, the more inwardly frustrated he became.

The rule that was good in itself tore him up inside. It seemed that he could never again have that innocent wholeness which had made him so alive as an infant.

The solution to this problem in Paul's terms is Jesus Christ our Lord. We must try a psychological translation, since that is where our understanding begins. Paul believed, and we agree, that the rule against coveting is a good one, so we can't solve the problem simply by approving of coveting. But we can see that if man is to have life, he has to become free from the cycle of struggling not to covet, coveting, and condemning himself for coveting. To do that he has to stand outside that whole cycle and adopt a different attitude toward it. He has to recognize that that is "where he's at," and that it is not a healthy place to be. He then has to see that the reason he's caught up in it is that it is so important to him to be a good person. He can see that deep down he has to believe that he is a good person in order to live with himself with any inner comfort or satisfaction. He doesn't like himself except as he conforms to his notion of goodness. But even when he understands himself, his insight does not change his condition.

Still, change can occur. He can experience himself as so fully loved, accepted, affirmed by another, that his need to win his own approval diminishes. Its power over him won't disappear, but in principle, we may say, it is broken. That is, there is another basis now for his self-acceptance and his inner comfort.

When this happens the whole situation changes. He still sees that coveting is wrong and that he continues to covet. But that no longer upsets him deeply. He can face the fact of his own failure to live up to his ideals about himself without becoming preoccupied with this failure. He is free to turn toward others, and to act in their behalf. In the process the actual coveting declines. He finds himself obeying the law.

At the psychological level, that is what I mean by the principle: "You don't have to be or do what you ought to be or do; therefore you are free to be or do it." You as a person, in your fundamental worth, are secure. Hence you should be under no psychological compulsion to prove yourself. When you appropriate that truth psychologically, you are free from the tensions that make the moral rules destructive. The rules remain, but you now find yourself conforming to these rules without pain and struggle. They express and describe what you want to be and do.

Paul did not have in mind the accepting love of another human being. And even when we approach this matter psychologically, we should not stop with that. The power of human love to free the neighbor should not be minimized, but it should not be exaggerated either. When is human love really without conditions? The vivid experience of a liberating love is so rare and precious that in our eagerness to retain it we may place ourselves in bondage to conditions, real or imagined, that we associate with it. Also no fellow human can know us in such a way that we can be sure that his acceptance includes everything about us, or that it will last.

Our need of acceptance, if we are to be freed from the pressure to prove or to justify ourselves, is total. The question I confront about myself finally is not whether what I am or do is acceptable to this person or that, although that matters greatly to me. It is whether what I am and do is acceptable. If it is not, then I cannot accept it, except by self-deceit, even if some other human being seems to accept it. If it is, then I can stand secure even if other human beings condemn me. If in order to be acceptable I must cease to covet, then I am caught in the cycle of self-preoccupation and misery that Paul described. If I am acceptable even in my coveting, then I can accept myself, transcend my coveting, and live.

Further than this psychology cannot go. It can describe the need to believe ourselves acceptable. It can teach us techniques by which we may try to persuade ourselves that we are acceptable. But it cannot announce that in fact we are acceptable.

For this very reason psychology sometimes cheats us here. It tries to enable us to accept ourselves by dulling our sensitivity to the moral law. It suggests that coveting is not, after all, so bad, since everyone covets. We are taught to accept ourselves by lowering the standards of expectation.

There are expectations that many of us have internalized from which we do indeed need to be freed. We have been taught to condemn sexual desires that should not be condemned. Christians have sometimes thought that they should be free of hostile and negative feelings in ways which could only lead to unhealthy repression. Hence we are indebted to the psychologists who have helped us to understand the distorted forms that the law has taken.

But there are true moral principles to which we should not dull our sensitivity. We *should* act so as to contribute to justice and peace. We *should* avoid involving ourselves in the exploitation of the less privileged. We *should* act now so that the conditions on this planet for our children and our grandchildren will be healthy and hopeful. We *should* become more aware of the feelings of others and deal more openly with them. We *should* love our neighbors as ourselves.

If we sensitively attend to these laws, they will affect us in much the way that Paul described himself as affected by the law against coveting. They, too, will destroy the spontaneous life within us. Insofar as we try to deal with this destructiveness by weakening our seriousness about the laws, we seek our own health at the expense of the neighbor. These laws, in Paul's terms, are holy, just, and good. But they condemn us and destroy us.

In the face of moral laws like these how can we believe that we are acceptable? It cannot be on the basis of our innocence, for none of us are innocent. It cannot be on the basis that we have met standards for acceptability. The man of sensitive conscience knows that he has not. And it is not sufficient that a fellow human being accept us, valuable and helpful as that is.

As I have wrestled recently with this problem, I have been helped by some comments of a friend, Lauren Ekroth, who is deeply involved in several forms of the human potential move-

ment. He said that in order to receive benefits from these methods of human development, it is necessary at first to rely upon
the experience and wisdom of the leader. But in the end, when
insight and understanding have come, or when new wholeness
and strength are experienced, a person finds that they are his
own. They well up within from depths he did not know he had.
The sense of deriving these benefits from the teacher turns out
to be an illusion.

So it is with the acceptance that frees a man from the need
to justify himself. He seems to experience it in the words and
gestures of another person. But finally, if it is real, it turns out
to be within himself, independent of the imperfections of a
fellowman's acceptance. It wells up within him from depths he
did not know he had—from the depths where God is.

The basic task of the church is to announce and realize God's
free acceptance. It does so by being itself an accepting and
affirming community. But it does so more fundamentally by
pointing, through word and sacrament, to the reality that it
serves and from which it lives.

To be faithful, however, the church must affirm acceptance
in a way that does not dull the sensitivity of our consciences. It
continues to make us aware of the legitimate demand of true
righteousness. We are not freed from the consciousness that we
are often, even continuously, in the wrong. The church's task is
rightly to balance grace and law.

Herbert Braun recently retired from an illustrious career as
a professor of New Testament at the University of Mainz. Once
when he preached at the leading Protestant church in that city
he attacked the congregation for having come to church. He
urged that they should be out on the golf courses, enjoying
themselves.

That was a dramatic way of preaching grace. Braun believed
that many of those who attended church did so out of the belief
that faithful churchmanship helped them to become acceptable
people. Certainly that has been a widespread reason for supporting churches. Church attendance is felt to be a particularly

meritorious kind of action that may compensate for some of the compromises with which daily life and business are filled. Insofar as that is the reason for coming to church, Braun is right. The man who has heard the gospel will know that he does not need to support the church. But if Braun meant that the one who had truly understood the gospel would in fact not come to church, then I think he was wrong. The man who is freed from the supposition that church attendance is a way of gaining merit and of justifying himself will ordinarily support the institution which bears that message.

Carl Michalson used to make the same point about prayer. The Christian, he said, doesn't need to pray. In the pietistic circles of Methodism that sounded strange. I grew up thinking that the more I prayed, the better; that prayer was the means of becoming what I should become. But Michalson was right. If one uses prayer as a means of meeting the requirements of acceptability, then prayer becomes an enemy of the Christian message that we are accepted already. On the other hand, Michalson was not attacking prayer. The Christian, he said, is at liberty to pray. He does not live under obligation but under freedom. He may approach God whenever he wishes and chooses.

The meaning of grace goes still farther. It touches us in the very ground of our being at that point of gnawing anxiety about ourselves which is deeper than all the particular worries and fears in which we express it. How much of my behavior, and I suspect of yours as well, is to be explained by this deep-seated uneasiness that something is missing, something is lacking, something is insufficient. Sometimes I feel that if only I could get some idea across, publish one more book on just the right subject, or shape the minds of a few students in the appropriate way, then I would have accomplished something, be somebody, fulfill my mission in life. Sometimes in the face of the acute practical problems of the world, I feel instead that only by contributing to their solution can I justify myself, that is, can I be and do what I should be and do. Thus I am driven to work by a need that is deeper than fear or ambition.

Now, insofar as I heed the gospel, I find that I do not need to write books or engage in social action in order to justify my existence. But I do not necessarily stop writing or acting. I may instead find that I am freed to work better as my response to the grace by which I live.

There is a special irony that a discussion of grace may be peculiarly liable to communicate law instead. Suppose that you have found what I have said to be persuasive. How then do you react? If I were in your shoes, I would be inclined to engage in some self-criticism. How little I am open to grace! How hard I work to justify myself! And how barren are the results! I must work harder at living from grace and not from law! Alas! If grace becomes law, where can grace be found?

The good news is not that if we will meet certain conditions, open ourselves in a certain way, or give up trying to justify ourselves, God will then be gracious to us. The gospel is instead that God *is* gracious to us. Therefore we can be open and cease to try to justify ourselves. But whether we are open or not, whether we trust him or not, God is gracious. Indeed, God is nothing other than Grace itself.

10

The Faith That Kills and the Faith That Quickens

We live in a time when the four-letter words are "in" and the three-letter words, such as God and sin, are "out." Many people, even people in the churches, are uncomfortable with these words. They conjure up associations that are either incredible or objectionable, or both. In the presence of those for whom these words have such connotations, and their name is legion, I too am uncomfortable with them. But left to myself, in my personal understanding of reality, I find them useful and necessary. I believe that life is a gift and I can think of no better way to name the giver than "God." I find within myself that which blinds me to the possibilities of life and refuses to embody them even when I see them clearly, and I can think of no better way to speak of that than as sin.

Many of those who are no longer comfortable speaking of God and sin still speak much of faith. They find "faith" a word they can utter without embarrassment. Indeed, it is striking how central that word has become, as the word "God" fades to the margins.

I, on the contrary, hesitate before the word "faith." It means so many different things, and it is so easily used to conceal an absence of meaning. The common use of this slippery word falsely suggests agreement where there is none. And yet it is claimed that salvation itself depends upon what it names, or faith is even identified with salvation.

The reason for the excessive use of this word is that the Reformers, and especially Luther, discovered such rich meaning in it. To follow Luther has meant more than anything else to accept the slogan "justification by faith alone." Most of the greatest theologians of modern times have worked in the shadow of Luther.

The phrase "justification by faith alone" is not in the Bible. Even the phrase "justification by faith" is rare. It is one of several ways in which Paul makes the crucial point that we do not save ourselves by obedience to the law, but that instead God has done what was necessary through Christ.

However, faith is not just a narrowly Lutheran approach to justification. In some form it is crucial to religion in general and even to quasi-religious movements. To take a far-out example, consider the following quote from Ken Kesey as reported by Tom Wolfe in *The Electric Kool-Aid Acid Test*: " 'You've got to have some faith in what we're trying to do. It's easy to have faith as long as it goes along with what you already know. But you've got to have faith in us all the way. Somebody like Gleason —Gleason was with us this far.' Kesey spreads his thumb and forefinger about two inches apart. 'He was with us as long as our fantasy coincided with his. But as soon as we went on further, he didn't understand it, so he was against us. He had . . . no faith.' " (Bantam Books, Inc., edition, 1969, p. 27. The Farrar, Straus & Giroux, Inc., edition was published in 1968.)

But what is this faith for which both Martin Luther and Ken Kesey as well as many other religious leaders call? Is it the uncritical acceptance of someone else's authority? Certainly faith is closely associated in the popular mind with such authoritarianism, and Kesey's call for faith could even be understood in this sense. This is the worst fate that has befallen the idea, but it was and continues to be an almost inevitable development. Consider how it happened in Christianity.

In the first generation Christians witnessed to an event that

transformed their human condition and situation. Their lives
and communities supported the credibility of their witness. What
they said rang true to others. These people acted upon it, and
their initial confidence was reinforced. Their lives were reordered
around this new central fact and experience.

Believing the message was a matter of faith. Acting upon that
belief was a matter of faith. Remaining loyal to its implications
and living in the community of those who believed was a matter
of faith. There was authority aplenty here, but there was no
authoritarianism.

However, as time passed the situation inevitably changed. The
Christian community settled down to become one among others.
Its claims became one set of teachings alongside others. The
reasonable man asked evidence or proof. Why should one accept
Christ rather than another?

It is to the church's credit that on the whole it accepted the
challenge and tried intelligently to explain itself. Sometimes it
succeeded in persuading an honest inquirer that what it taught
made more sense than any other teaching available. He might
then become a Christian. But the church could not exist as an
assembly of individuals whose reason had led them to more or
less similar conclusions. The church had a received truth that it
could not submit to a popular vote. The received doctrine had
the authority of the apostles, and the community used its own
authority to keep its members faithful to this doctrine. Faith
came to mean the acceptance of the authority of the apostles
based upon acceptance of the authority of the community. What
was believed by faith was what the community understood the
apostles to have taught.

The local community became more and more a part of a
larger institution. Authority moved from the community to the
inclusive church and its officers. If this had not occurred, the
many communities would have drifted into hopeless diversity.
But when it occurred, the shift to authoritarianism became complete. Decisions about what is to be believed are made for one

by distant and unknown persons many of whom are long dead. One must believe because the institution requires belief. Penalties for not believing as one should arise and are enforced by social pressure, by the church, and even at times by the state. Faith becomes acceptance of what one finds implausible on the grounds of an external and coercive authority. Nothing could be farther from the New Testament! Yet no development from the New Testament could be more natural!

Luther did much to distinguish saving faith from the acceptance of beliefs on authority. Faith was for him a deeply inward and personal appropriation for oneself of the promise of God. It involved all of man's faculties. But this faith still presupposed the objective reliability of the Bible. The acceptance of that reliability became the ground for a new authoritarianism in which a book was substituted for an institution. The repeated efforts of Christian thinkers to avoid the association of faith with that authoritarianism have been only partly successful.

We can understand why authoritarian belief arises. We can see that it helps to maintain the unity of the church, and that, when the belief is sane and positive, it helps many individuals to have healthy and fruitful lives. There is comfort and relief in letting someone else do one's thinking for one. And if one is in any case not going to work out his own beliefs, there are good reasons for turning the task over to the Catholic Church or the Bible rather than to many of the other willing masters that are around.

Even so, authoritarian belief is alien to the genius of Christianity. It even contradicts it. Authoritarian belief is simply the occurrence within our tradition of a fate that tends to overcome all traditions which survive the vitality of their childhood. Authoritarian belief blocks freedom, openness, and the quest for truth. It is the faith that kills.

Alongside this deadening form of faith there are others that quicken. The term for faith most commonly set over against authoritarian belief is trust. There is no question that trust quickens. I treated trust at some length in the chapter on "Trusting and Deciding." But quickening faith takes still other forms as well. We shall briefly consider six.

1. One meaning of faith is more clearly expressed as faithfulness. The man of faith is loyal, trustworthy, steadfast. He keeps faith with others. His word counts. His yes is yes, and his no, no. His behavior conforms to his assertions, and his assertions conform to his convictions. He endures in adverse circumstances. He is true to himself and true to his friends.

Faithfulness is exalted in the New Testament and in the Christian tradition. But faith in this sense is exalted everywhere. There is little that is distinctively Christian about it.

2. Another phenomenon that is sometimes called faith is life-affirmation. When after many catastrophes a man picks up the pieces of life and begins again, we say he has great faith. We do not mean that he is confident that all will go well. He knows better than that. We do not mean that he holds firmly to particular beliefs. Whatever he once believed may now be shattered. But he refuses to be beaten. He stands again on his feet. He does what is necessary.

I doubt that this kind of life-affirmation is ever in view in the New Testament. But in a broader sense, as we compare our Judeo-Christian heritage with other traditions we do see that it is a life-affirming one. It asserts that life as such is good despite all suffering. Hence it grounds also the response of affirming one's own life even in the most adverse circumstances. But moving as this is, it is not what the gospel is about.

3. A third type of faith is the spirit of confidence in another. This is primary in Jesus' use of faith. If in confrontation with him a person was utterly confident that he could be healed, then healing came. Jesus would say, "Your faith has made you whole."

Utter confidence, whether in another person or in God, is a powerful force. There is no reason to be skeptical of Jesus' assertion that men and women were healed by it, even dramatically healed of decidedly physical diseases. Our understanding of these matters is still in its infancy, but there are several lines of contemporary experience and inquiry that suggest that in the future men will recognize a still closer interconnection of psychological and physical forces and a still greater possibility for changes in the psyche to affect powerfully the condition of the body. Confidence of the kind inspired by Jesus may even have an effect on the world outside one's body. It would be dangerous to set any limit on the supernormal or miraculous changes effected by such confidence.

But confidence of this sort is not a specifically Christian phenomenon. It is evoked by other charismatic figures besides Jesus, both within and without the Christian community. On the other hand, many Christians lack any experience of such confidence and of the supernormal events associated with it. In our time of spiritual poverty, we tend to gape at such events, to be incredulous, and, if persuaded of their reality, to make much of them. But Paul rightly treated them as among the lesser gifts of the spirit. We may hope that the time will come when we can follow Paul here.

This kind of confidence is a valuable and positive force, and it usually works for good. But it is a serious mistake to identify it or its consequences with what is fundamental to Christian life.

For most of us most of the time the possibility of such confidence plays a paradoxical role. My parents are members of a prayer fellowship. On one occasion the fellowship prayed for several weeks for a young woman lost on a mountain in Baja California. She was found safe, and she fully recovered in a short time. My parents assured me that no one was more surprised than were the members of the prayer fellowship.

Clearly they were asking divine aid without expecting it. Would it be better to maintain, in the face of all contrary probabilities, an attitude of utter confidence that whatever we ask of God he will give us? Surely not! If we want to move mountains, we had better stick to bulldozers. It is a perversion of the gospel to suppose that the person who dies of cancer suffers because of lack of faith. It is well to remember that Paul three times asked for the removal of some irritant, and that his request was not granted. There is no particular virtue in working ourselves into special states of mind in our efforts to be confident that something will happen.

4. In the fourth place, "faith" is sometimes used to refer to our basic way of experiencing the world. Let's call that our vision of reality. By vision I don't mean simply sense experience through the eyes. I don't mean visions either. Nor do I mean our explicit theories about the world, our world views, although that comes closer. A world view articulates a vision of reality more or less adequately, but the vision itself underlies and precedes the articulation. Much of it is usually unconscious. It is made up of elements that are so self-evident to us that it would ordinarily not occur to us to state them. Our vision of reality is the system of unquestioned presuppositions in relation to which other ideas appear as plausible or stupid.

However, our vision of reality can change. One way this happens is by verbally expressing heretofore unconscious assumptions and examining them alongside alternative assumptions. In such comparisons certainty about them is sometimes shattered.

Christianity is not bound up with any one world view, but it cannot be entirely separated from a vision of reality. That is, there are basic ways of perceiving the world that simply don't fit the gospel. For example, if a man thinks of reality entirely as what is seen, heard, smelled, tasted, and touched, the needs to which the gospel speaks are not even recognized. The vision of reality of the Judeo-Christian community centers on personal subjects and their interrelationships, and these are not visible through the sense organs. Or if one perceives the world as made up of inexorable forces that by pure necessity work out their effects, then the responsibility which Christianity attributes to persons cannot be acknowledged. Or if one perceives all things as equally good or bad, recognizing no distinctions of better or worse, then the concerns for justice and peace, so central to Christianity, become nonsensical.

The Judeo-Christian vision of a reality in which personal subjects are of central importance, and in which they are responsible for what they do in relation to possibilities of good and evil, has been held by many people who did not call themselves Jews or Christians. They adopted it without thinking, simply as common sense. They have even employed it to criticize Christian teaching. Hence the gospel could be proclaimed in a context in which it made sense. Questions of philosophy or world view could be set aside.

Today, however, other visions of reality are challenging and displacing the Christian one. Traditional expressions of the Christian vision are crumbling and cannot be restored. The question of the future of Christianity and the question of world view have again become entangled. Faith in the sense of a vision of reality is important for the gospel.

But, of course, the gospel is not the proclamation of a world view. Originally it both presupposed and changed the vision of reality that it found. Today it must do the same. There is nowhere to begin except where people are. The gospel must be spoken in a way that makes sense. If it is, it can open the way toward a new, more congenial vision of reality, while theologians and philosophers pave the way with new insights and generalizations.

5. When the gospel is effectively heard it changes not only the way a person perceives reality but also the way he is. It changes his mode of existence. Theologians have increasingly directed attention to this Christian mode of existence and identified it with faith.

One reason for this trend in recent times is that the beliefs, and even the vision of reality associated with Christianity, have become doubtful. That seems to undercut also the grounds of faithfulness and the possibility of confidence. But the occurrence of a distinctive way of being is better understood today than ever before, thanks to the rise of existentialism.

Rudolf Bultmann has shown us that the modern philosophical understanding of authentic existence illumines Christian faith. Paul Tillich has described the new being as that mode of exist-

ence in which to participate is to have faith. Building on their
work, others have described how Christianity has heightened
man's sense of responsibility for himself and of the gulf between
his best deeds, thoughts, and motives and that which he is responsible to be and do. It held up a new ideal of love and at the
same time brought into being a way of life in which that love was
both needed and possible.

To use the word "faith" to name the distinctively Christian
existence is legitimate. But it is not free from problems. Many
who sincerely believe in Christ as their savior participate very
little in this way of being. Others who reject Christianity embody
this mode of existence more fully. On the other hand, keeping
faith in this sense alive is not as independent of doubtful beliefs
as its advocates sometimes suppose. It may be clearer to think of
Christian existence as an outgrowth of faith rather than as itself
the one, key meaning of faith.

6. The contemporary German theologian Gerhard Ebeling
has taught us to think of faith in still another way, which is the
sixth and last we will consider in this chapter. Faith, he says, is
certainty. When I first read that, I was put off by it. Certainty is
bound up in my mind with particular beliefs, and I am suspicious
of those who claim to be certain about anything. But that is not
at all what Ebeling means. "Certainty" is the translation of
Gewissheit, and a better translation in this case would be "assuredness." Traditionally we have spoken of assurance, but that
too suggests that we are sure about something, whereas Ebeling
speaks of a state of being in which we find ourselves grounded,
established, or, in traditional language, justified. The man who
is assured is free for what comes, free for the future, free for his
neighbor. He is free to follow truth wherever it leads him.

Ebeling believes that this is the gift of the gospel. When the
Christian message is rightly spoken it establishes the one who
hears, that is, it makes him an assured person. Indeed, the
Christian word is the word that accomplishes that result, whatever words are used in the speaking.

As I have reflected over this formulation of Ebeling to which

I first responded negatively, I have decided that he does indeed come close to the mark. Of course, no early Christian would have put his thought in this way. And to me it seems that this is only one part of what the gospel does and cannot become the criterion of the whole. But the gospel does accomplish this to the extent that it is truly heard, and of all that it does, nothing could be more important than this. Whether or not we call it "faith," we must learn how to speak of assuredness, and more important, how to make it a reality.

Even so, assuredness is not the heart of the gospel. It is at most the heart of what the gospel accomplishes. The gospel is not about faith in any of these senses. The gospel is about grace. The gospel tells us what grace has done, and in the light of that we can discern what it is doing now. We are free to talk about that, to be critical even of the ways in which the New Testament describes it, to use whatever language most clearly communicates what we find. We are free to call it all faith, but we are also free to use other terms. Our effort to understand what grace does is a response to grace in which we can see the working of grace. We can learn much from the history of past efforts to describe what grace does, but we have much yet to learn.

So, in conclusion, let me say: be faithful, affirm life, have confidence, stand fast in a Christian vision of reality, enter more deeply into Christian existence, be assured. But do not be disturbed if your experience does not fit these concepts. You are not required to have faith in any of these senses. All forms of quickening faith are gifts. Grace works in us freely and according to its own purposes. Be glad, for you have been given much.

11

Pandora's Box

As a child I remember reading the story of Pandora and her box in *The Book of Knowledge*. In that account, after all the terrible ills of mankind had escaped from the box, Pandora slammed it shut. A small voice pleaded to be allowed to escape. It was hope. Pandora relented, and thus hope entered the world to counterbalance all the evils and make them endurable.

Later I discovered that such an interpretation was probably false to the story's original intention. The meaning there may have been that hope is the last and worst of the evils. As long as men hope for something, they are victims of disappointment and disillusionment. Only when hope is abandoned can one adjust to reality and achieve what happiness is possible for man.

Those two interpretations represent basic alternative visions of reality. In one, man lives from his anticipations of a future. In the other, he accepts the course of events as they come, expecting nothing more. In our culture, and within us individually, these two visions struggle for dominance.

Christianity is on the side of hope. We were reminded of this recently by a whole spate of books of which the best-known is Jürgen Moltmann's *The Theology of Hope*. Against the neo-orthodox and existentialist tendency to focus on the present moment as the time of encounter and decision, Moltmann and others have stressed that the present has its meaning in its relation to the future. Hope is necessary if one is to muster the energies needed to say "No!" to injustice and meaningless suffering.

Most of our conscious hope focuses on short-term goals. We are motivated by the hope of winning a game, getting a job, or shortening a war. Reinhold Niebuhr taught us to hope for the resolution of particular social problems—for example, the achievement of a balance of power between capital and labor. Niebuhr knew that success in that area would lead to new problems, but that did not lessen its importance. We do not need to believe in utopia in order to work for justice and peace today.

On other hand, what we believe about the larger context of our efforts makes a difference. Over the longer haul hope invests itself strongly in winning the game, getting the job, shortening the war, and achieving economic justice only if these seem to add up to something enduring. Consciously or unconsciously our particular short-term hopes give evidence of a deeper hope that the passing parade of events really matters, that it makes a difference to God himself.

That our hope is finally that we can make a contribution to God does not reduce the importance of what we believe about history. On the contrary. How we view the historical situation affects our hope all the more because what happens matters also to God.

To act zestfully for justice I need to believe both that some approximation of justice is possible in the particular situation and also that the attainment of justice can pave the way for other values. I will have little hope for the liberation of the Third World peoples if I believe that their revolutions have no chance of success. Even if I see military and political success as possible, I will have little enthusiasm if the liberated peoples can anticipate nothing but misery. This is the threat implicit in the warnings of ecologists and environmentalists. Their warnings pose a crisis for hope of unparalleled proportions, and I want to tell how this crisis has affected me.

Since World War II we have known that man had weapons with which he could destroy life on the planet. This awareness together with the expectation that man would sooner or later use these weapons cast a pall over the lives of many sensitive persons. But I realize now that I did not really believe that man would destroy himself with these weapons. Rationally I saw the danger, but deep down I felt that man would refrain from this final outrage.

The environmental crisis, however, poses a different kind of problem. In order to avoid self-destruction through atomic, chemical, or bacterial weapons, we have only to refrain from certain actions that we are quite clear about. But to avoid the horrors of environmental catastrophe, we must make radical changes in our way of living, and we do not yet even have a clear idea of what those changes should be. I can believe that men will refrain from consciously precipitating their immediate destruction. I find it hard to believe that men will pay the price in change now to avoid conditions which will make catastrophe inevitable later.

Let me explain. I will follow the projections of the research team at the Massachusetts Institute of Technology under the leadership of Jay Forrester and Dennis Meadows. They employed modern computer technology in order to project the interaction of basic world trends. The results are, to put it mildly, frightening, so frightening that most people find it more comfortable to ignore them.

The problem is the likelihood of overshoot and collapse of human population on a world scale. Although population growth in some places is slowing down, worldwide, it continues unabated. Because so many of the people now alive are young, rapid continued growth is inevitable. Doubling time worldwide, apart from catastrophes far greater than any that have occurred in recent centuries, is likely to be about thirty-five years.

Almost everyone agrees that world population cannot continue to double indefinitely three times a century. To project it as doing so leads to ridiculous conclusions. Just two hundred years from now the Hawaiian Islands would have to support fifty million people. China would have a population of fifty billion. We all assume that population growth will come under control before those figures are reached. We usually suppose that we can leave this for later generations to work out. But the projections of the MIT studies indicate that even one more doubling is not likely to be possible. That is a different matter. At this point we are talking about what population pressures will do within the lifetime of many of us.

The MIT projection is that if we continue on our way as at present, shortages of resources for industry will slow population growth within twenty years and stop it, early in the twenty-first century, at approximately six billion. They will then cause a fifty-year decline to a total world population of two billion people. Such a dying off of two thirds of the people on the planet is not pleasant to contemplate.

Suppose, then, that we are sensible enough to conserve our resources more carefully, and especially to recycle everything we can. That will stretch out available resources over a much longer period of time. It will allow population to rise higher, although still not to double its present figure. But in this case, early in the twenty-first century will come a pollution crisis that will destroy in a few years five sixths of the world's population!

If we employ our ingenuity to control pollution to a degree beyond any we now anticipate, then population will rise further still, only to be stopped by terrible famines later in the next century. The only projection that does not lead to catastrophe is the quite impossible one of immediately stabilizing population and industry on a worldwide basis at present levels. That could be done only by methods none of us would condone. Unless survival can be with dignity and decency, unless there can be some prospect of a good life in a good society, perhaps it is better that the whole human experiment end soon.

These projections are bleak enough, but they leave many dangers out of account. I am sufficiently optimistic to believe that men may refrain from destroying the planet with atomic and bacterial weapons under ordinary circumstances. I am not sufficiently optimistic to think that if two thirds of us Americans were dying for lack of resources, we would fail to use our weapons to extract such resources from other, more favored, nations. Environmental catastrophe would almost certainly provoke a final and totally destructive war.

The basic point is that, in order to produce catastrophes we need only to continue to think and act as we now think and act. That is all too easy. In the past we have supposed that present economic development enhanced the prospects for our children and grandchildren. We did not have to choose between our enjoyment of the world's resources and their chance for a good life. Even now, as the threat becomes clearer, we still refuse to face the moral issue on any large scale.

When we confront this picture, the problem of hope becomes a very pressing one. One possibility is to fall back upon what some people call—wrongly, I think—faith in God. One can suppose that God will not let anything so terrible happen, that he will intervene to prevent it. Against such a view the Jews rightly remind us that God did not prevent Auschwitz.

A second possibility is to give up. That need not be so bad. Catastrophes of great magnitude may not occur in this century. By the time our style of life has made the planet unfit for human habitation, we will be dead. Louis XIV is reported to have said, *"Après moi, le déluge."* That might be the slogan of our generation. If catastrophe is inevitable, eat, drink, and be merry. But I cannot in fact adopt that attitude either. I have been shaped too deeply by my Christian heritage.

My actual response has been to look for alternatives. That search expresses hope. Without arguing with the projections, I have believed that there may be some ways of warding off, or at least of mitigating, catastrophe, ways that, if clarified, men might adopt in time. Perhaps there are steps we could take, steps that would appeal to persons for many reasons, and that, if taken, would save our children and grandchildren from destruction. Perhaps there is some way in which short-run self-interest for our generation could be made coincident with the interests of our descendants in the next century.

If population increase by itself were the cause of catastrophe, the situation would be hopeless. Population growth cannot be halted without catastrophe within the next century. But this is not the case. Increasing consumption of goods, land, and energy is the more fundamental threat. The discouraging problem is that an increasing population could level off its consumption only if each person consumed less, whereas all our habits and traditions point to rapidly increasing per capita consumption. Voluntary asceticism does not appear likely to effect the needed change.

Since so much of the world's consuming is done by Americans, we have a special responsibility to deal with this dilemma. Could we, while trying to bring the growth of population under control by humane methods, also develop life-styles that would give more satisfaction to people while reducing consumption? Could we develop an economy that would better distribute goods and work while operating at a slower pace and allowing for more enjoyable leisure? If so, then the changes would not involve a net sacrifice. The threat to man's survival could even function as a prod to develop a saner and a happier society.

When the problem is put in this way, hope is strengthened. The achievement of such a goal, although difficult, and even unlikely, is not impossible. It is worth the try. Hope does not require advance assurance of success.

An adequate blueprint for action must be many-sided, experimental, pluralistic, and open-ended. No one has all the answers. I shall discuss just one piece of the answer, a piece that has encouraged me in my hopeful quest to find reasons for hope.

One of the ironic features of our present situation is that we are very prosperous, consuming at a great rate, but feeling rather poor, too poor to respond vigorously to the needs of our own people for decent housing, adequate food and medical care, good education for children, and protection from violent abuse. Part of the reason is that our desire for comforts and luxuries is insatiable. But part of the reason is also that so much of our consumption adds nothing to our enjoyment of life. The most glaring example has been the staggering waste involved in our destructive war in Vietnam. But there are others.

Men who once walked to work now own expensive automobiles and use vast amounts of gasoline to spend an hour driving to work over fabulously expensive freeways. As measured by gross national product this is progress. Walking to work added only a few cents to the GNP for the shoe leather used. Now many a man spends five to ten dollars a day for driving and parking and then spends more money at a gym or golf course to get the exercise he misses by not walking. He has and spends a lot more money than he once did. In that sense he is richer. But he may have no more left to spend on what he really enjoys, and he now wastes two hours a day on freeway driving. If people could get their exercise walking to work in pleasant surroundings, surely this reduction of consumption would not be experienced as sacrifice.

For that to happen, cities would have to be built in a quite different way. But they *can* be built in that different way. The whole phenomenon of urban and suburban sprawl with its extreme waste and costliness can be reversed. The life that would ensue would be pleasanter. No reduction would be necessitated in enjoyable consumption. Is it not possible that people might be lured by its attractiveness into taking a step like this that would at the same time make possible life and happiness for our descendants?

Dependence upon wasteful and unpleasant transportation is not the only problem with our present cities. They eat up farmland that will one day be urgently needed for the production of food. They create a wretched environment for the poor whom we crowd into their centers. Goods and services become increasingly difficult to provide. Tensions are generated that erupt in violence and destruction which only worsen conditions for the wretched.

I personally found a new surge of hope through my encounter with Paolo Soleri. He has meditated for years on the conditions of our cities, and he has envisioned new cities. He calls them architectural ecologies, or arcologies. These would relate people to one another in far more human ways while greatly reducing the present waste of resources. The arcologies that he proposes are beautiful to behold, brilliant in design, and, best of all, technologically and economically possible.

It may be that in promoting the work of one visionary architect I am moving away from my role as theologian. But I do not think so. Our basic belief, that is, our theology, must express itself in the concrete reality of our life or it is phony. If one thinks he believes in God or in freedom for his fellowman, while being unaffected thereby in his daily activities and in the way he votes on election day, then he is deceiving himself. He is playing games with ideas. He does not believe what he supposes that he believes. Similarly, when we design a building or a city, it expresses what we really believe, what we really prize, the way we really live.

Most architects, certainly the great ones, know this. There is more theology in the writings of architects than in that of any other profession. Certainly Soleri is no exception. He is inspired by Teilhard de Chardin. He sees the task of the city as facilitating what Teilhard called convergence. That is, having spread out over the whole globe, men must now come together in new dimensions and intensities of interaction. Our new frontiers are not at the fringes of spatial expansion. Even our exploration of the solar system can only be a side issue. Our new frontiers are to be found in our relationships with each other. Soleri is designing cities that would help to open up new possibilities of creative community.

I know, of course, and I suppose that Soleri knows, that his arcologies may not work. First, they may not be tried. Second,

if they are tried, they may turn out to produce new and un-
foreseen problems so serious that they must be abandoned. Neither I nor anyone can be certain that any particular program
will achieve its goals.

But certainty is not necessary for effective hope. What is required is some image of what might work. My general conviction that there must be some way through the morass grows
weak if I cannot find even one plausible suggestion. The spirit
of hope needs concrete, if provisional, forms.

The degree of our need for hope is a function of the seriousness with which we take the threats to man's well-being. But it
is also true that the seriousness with which we take these threats
is partly a function of our hope. A man of little hope cannot face
the threats. It is necessary for him to deny or belittle them. Better
to refuse to face reality than to be overwhelmed by despair. But
the man whose basic hopefulness is strong can hear the dangers
openly and then enter into the difficult but creative task of finding a way through.

Whether we have basic hope is partly a matter of our genes
and of our early environment. But it is also bound up with our
ultimate convictions about the world. It depends upon where we
look to get our clues to the nature of the whole. If we look at
the many acts of narrow self-interest that characterize so much
of our society, we may conclude that men are, after all, self-
centered beings who act and think and dream only to gain their
private ends. Or if we note primarily the ways that, out of sheer
habit or stupidity, men fail to rise even to the demands of self-
interest, we will have plenty of evidence that inertia rules the
world. In either case, we will have little reason to be hopeful as
to man's prospects.

It is possible, however, to notice another characteristic of human behavior. At times men heed truth even when it is painful.
At times, for the sake of their children or even their friends, they
undertake difficult and painful tasks. At times, they envision a
better world and are moved to act by their vision even when
they know they will themselves have no part in it.

Christianity urges us to attend both to the inertia and to the narrow self-interest, which it calls sin, and to the transcending concern for truth and for others, in which it discerns the Spirit that is Holy. Some Christians have thought the former too ugly and have wanted to declare men virtuous. The result has been to view life unrealistically, to expect of it what it does not afford, to fail to deal prudently with the actual possibilities of our life together. Other Christians have seen only the clash of interests and the resistance to the creative new. They have grown cynical and have despaired of this life, sometimes directing their hope to another world.

Christian hope, on the other hand, sustains a balance. It recognizes sin in others, and especially in oneself. It perceives the destructive consequences to which inertia and narrow self-interest lead. But it sees also that something else is happening, that new insights arise, that men are touched by conscience, that the plight of others moves many to generosity. As long as that is true, we have no right to despair. And that is always true. For God is not dead.

12

Christ as the Image of Love

In *One Flew Over the Cuckoo's Nest,* Ken Kesey portrays a modern-day embodiment of the Greek god Dionysus, the god of wine and vitality, being transformed into a Christ figure. It is a novel vision. I wish I could believe it to be a foretaste of things to come.

The story is located in a men's ward in a mental hospital. The ward is presided over by a castrating nurse whose rule ensures that the weak and cowardly men under her supervision will never gain the confidence they need. Into that ward comes a small-time card shark who found it more convenient to be sentenced to an asylum than to jail for his petty misdeeds. This man, McMurphy by name, is thoroughly sure of himself, out for profit and pleasure, and fully capable of enjoying what he gets. His contagious vitality is a threat to the nurse, and her enmity is great, but he manages to stay just within the bounds that save him from overt punishment.

The punishment that the men fear is electric shock therapy. As long as they are quiet and orderly, they are safe. But if they become violent, the nurse can send them for treatment, and will send them repeatedly, as long as they resist her will.

McMurphy's Dionysian presence is enough to bring new life to the ward, but it is not enough to give the men the courage to leave. He is their hero, but as long as they see in all his actions the motive of self-interest, he cannot save them. Recognizing this, McMurphy changes. He uses physical violence to stop the bullying of the cruel ward attendants. He knows that that means the dreaded shock treatment, but he does not give in. He continues to resist the nurse for the sake of the others, accepting the repeated punishment until he is destroyed as a man. In kindness, one of the other men then smothers him in his sleep.

McMurphy, the man for himself, became the man for others. He suffered voluntarily for the sake of the men on the ward. Lest anyone miss the point, Kesey tells us that on the instrument of torture McMurphy's arms were outstretched.

In our recent history, too, there has been a Christ figure. His name is Martin Luther King. King assumed great responsibilities for the sake of his fellow blacks. But he went beyond that. He assumed responsibility for the whole nation. It was the nation's soul for which he sacrificed, both in the way he led the black movement and in his unequivocal opposition to the war in Vietnam. He knew that his way of nonviolent resistance was a dangerous one. He had premonitions of his own death. But he did not falter. When the assassin's bullet struck him down, there was a spontaneous recognition that here was one who represented Christ in our time.

The central element in the Christ figure is vicarious suffering. When a man gives his life freely for the sake of other people, we see Christ in him.

But such utter self-sacrifice cannot be the goal of ordinary Christian life. Indeed, it was not the goal of Jesus or King or the fictional McMurphy. It is far better if one can serve others and live, indeed, if one can enjoy serving others and be served by them as well. When we picture the goal for mankind it is surely not a world in which everyone is dying for everyone else's sake! It is a world in which mutual love fulfills all. The man who desires to die a martyr's death is not a Christian hero. He is simply sick.

However, while wanting to suffer for others is sick, willing-

ness to suffer if need be is Christian. Dying for others is the
extreme possibility that is entailed in loving them. We see the
full meaning of love when it leads to death in this way. Martin
Luther King was not a better Christian when he died than while
he lived. But the full meaning of his life became clearer.

The love that is expressed in this willingness even to die for
others is called in the New Testament *agapē*. It is a very special
kind of love. The word *agapē* was not much used in pre-Christian
speech. For that very reason it could become a technical term
by which Christians named what they found to be new and particular about their relation to one another and to other men.
They found that they were able to care for others without the
self-reference that is involved in most forms of love. And of
course in Jesus they saw this special kind of caring ideally embodied.

Although the Christian idea of love has become familiar, almost banal, its peculiarity has to be stressed again in each generation. There are many other forms of love, and English is poor
in its capacity to differentiate. Hence Christian love gets too easily confused with other kinds of love.

To distinguish Christian love from other forms is not to disparage the others or to say that the Christian does not have them
too. It is only to say that whereas the Christian experiences many
forms of love there is one that he associates especially with
Christ and with his response to Christ.

All forms of love are in some measure spontaneous. One may
go through the motions required by some form of love without
loving. But love has to happen to us. We cannot command it.

Generally love arises in relation either to some need we feel
or in relation to some attractiveness of the object. We love those
things and persons which minister to our hungers and strong
desires. We take pleasure in them and long for them when they
are absent. That is healthy and good. Sometimes, apart from any
prior felt need, we encounter something or someone that is beautiful or excellent. We are struck by admiration and affection.
That too is healthy and good.

We realize today more keenly than ever that many things can block the healthy freedom of these kinds of love. We can be so concerned about our own virtue that we inhibit spontaneous feeling toward others. When we repress our feelings of anger, we suppress also our feelings of affection and tenderness. If we try to control our action too tightly by our rational will, others do not feel warmth from us. These are important lessons. By becoming more comfortable about ourselves and all our feelings we can become more generous and outgoing toward others. Surely this is desired by Christians as much as by anyone.

Even so, this is not the distinctive form of Christian love, *agapē*. The self-reference remains. We love what meets our needs and what attracts us. This does not mean that we are calculating the consequences to ourselves of our love. If we were, that would not be love at all. But what the other does for us determines how we feel about him.

Agapē, on the other hand, is free from this self-reference. One loves the other for the other's sake. How much one loves him is not proportional to how much he meets one's need or to his attractiveness. The examples of *agapē* that make this clearest are those of love to the despised and outcast. Anders Nygren even defined *agapē* as a downward movement of love, that is, as directed toward the inferior. But that is surely wrong. Christian love can be directed toward those who fulfill our needs and attract us as well. The problem is that in that relation it is hard to distinguish the concern for the other in his otherness and the concern for him as he is related to the one who loves. Only where the other meets none of the Christian's needs and is naturally threatening or repulsive to him can *agapē* be readily sorted out and recognized. When *agapē* leads to suffering and death for the other's sake, we have the vivid example that represents Christ.

If we suppose that love must entail strong positive emotion, then the Christian ideal of *agapē* for all men becomes not only impossible but silly. There will always be cases in which other persons arouse negative emotions in us. Those cases are the ones in which the presence or absence of *agapē* is most clearly tested. Can we genuinely, with real concern and caring, desire and actively seek the good for those who make us feel uncomfortable, who are physically revolting to us, who have all the goods we lack and think we deserve, whose complacency exasperates us, whose criticism threatens our self-esteem, or who simply rub us the wrong way? To whatever extent we can meet this test, *agapē* is present in us.

Agapē is not unreal or impossible. But it rarely dominates our being or governs our action. When we are honest about why we have acted as we have, we rarely can think that *agapē* has been decisive. There are all sorts of other motives, such as wanting to live up to our own image of ourselves as Christians, that corrupt *agapē* even in our nobler actions. Such honesty is difficult, but it is important. A main function of Christian prayer and spiritual discipline is to attain it.

However, we should not be so preoccupied with motive that we neglect the action. A friend once said that he could rarely send a CARE package since he realized that he did so to salve his conscience. My reaction was that for whatever reason he sent the food, it would still feed a hungry family. We should act as *agapē* requires whether or not *agapē* motivates the act.

Agapē is closely bound up with action. It is oriented toward the future rather than toward the past. It seeks to achieve the well-being of its object, and this change of state has to be future-oriented. On the whole, this form of love has dominated the conception of love throughout Christian history. It is outgoing, assertive, and bound up with action.

Less central to the Christ figure in the past has been another form of love. I suspect that it will grow more prominent as time passes. It is fully grounded in Jesus.

In the New Testament this other form of love is called compassion. Today we name it better as empathy. Both mean "feeling with." Jesus had compassion for people, and the Christ figure has been associated with compassion throughout its history. But only recently have we realized how distinct is this form of love from *agapē,* how important in itself, and how badly needed in the Christian life.

In the past, compassion has sometimes been viewed as a ground or aspect of *agapē.* If we feel with others, then we will be actively concerned for their good. That is true. But we have often neglected the fact that compassion or empathy in and of itself is healing and redemptive. To know that one feels with us in our pain helps us to endure the pain. To know that one rejoices with us in our joy multiplies the joy. To feel the empathy of another for us is to be released from the bondage of unhealthy emotions.

Both the universal need for empathy and the slighting of it in the Christian tradition can be seen in the way that we have understood God. There has been universal agreement that God is *agapē.* He loves us without regard to our merits.

However, to assert that God has empathy for us is a highly controversial matter. Indeed, in the mainstream of the orthodox tradition it has been denied. To empathize with another is to be vulnerable, to be subject to his pain and suffering. God was understood to be impassible, that is, not subject to any injury or hurt. Therefore, he could not be viewed as sympathizing with us in our human misery. And insofar as the image of Christ was shaped in relation to this view of God, Christ too receded from man in such a way that men doubted his capacity for empathy. The cult of Mary grew up in Christendom partly because of the need to believe that there was one who understood.

Today we recognize that to empathize with others is a perfection we should not deny to God. If our clue to the nature of God is found in Jesus, then we must indeed affirm that God has compassion for us, that he shares with us both joy and sorrow.

Empathy relates to the past in much the way that *agapē* relates to the future. The feelings which one shares are those which the other *has* had, not those which he *will* have in the future. As *agapē* is actively oriented toward changing the future, so empathy is passively oriented toward receiving the past. And it turns out that this passive openness to the past has a power to change the future hardly less than the active direction of energies toward that end.

When empathy and *agapē* are combined in the Christ image, we have the vision of a new way of overcoming what is destructive about selfhood. We Westerners prize the selfhood from which Buddhism seeks to set us free. Yet we cannot deny the Buddhist analysis. My selfhood is bound up with insatiable craving. Also it separates me from you. However much we reach out to each other, a gulf remains. I am enclosed in my solitude; you, in yours. We hunger for each other, but we also resent and fear each other as threats and competitors. We see ourselves objectified by each other, used by each other, rejected by each other. In *No Exit,* Sartre places on the lips of his hero the now-famous phrase, "Hell is other people."

Christianity has strengthened selfhood more than has any other tradition. It has taught that through our relation to God we can endure the separation from each other. It has also taught that we can reach out to one another in concern and heal in some measure the sickness of our mutual isolation. But Sartre's existentialism shows that modern man has retained his isolated selfhood without the healing elements of groundedness in God and Christian love. Then, indeed, hell is other people. We can find happiness neither with them nor without them. All life becomes hell.

Christians today must face honestly this problem of the mutually isolating character of selfhood. We cannot solve it by simply reemphasizing our traditional teaching. We must incorporate that teaching but we must also go beyond it. Love can show us the way.

Empathy and *agapē* both challenge the final separateness of my self from other selves. If my feelings are shaped by empathy for others, then I receive their feelings into my experience on the same basis that I relate to my own past. If I have *agapē* for others as for myself, then my concern for the future of others becomes like my concern for my own future. Ideally I am no longer bound to a single line of inheritance from the past projected forward to my lonely death in the future. I live from others and for others. But not only so. In a community of empathy and *agapē* others live from me and for me as well. We become Christs to one another.

Obviously I am describing a state of affairs that is very distant from what we know. But we need such a vision in order to appraise what is now happening and to guide ourselves as Christians through the multiple possibilities now appearing for self-transformation and new types of relationship.

As long as individual selfhood is isolating and painful, there will be those who seek to escape it. The primordial eschatology of man is escape from self into unity with the all. Our dreams and visions are full of unions in which the self is lost in a larger whole.

Christianity has resisted this deep human longing in the name of the value of the individual person. In Christian eschatology the individual has been preserved as individual. He receives blessedness as an individual. There is a social dimension. But he is not reabsorbed with others into the original unity. The end is different from the beginning, enriched by the attainment of multiple personal selves.

Can Christianity maintain that commitment to the person? Our Western literature witnesses to the loss of selfhood. The widespread attraction of Eastern techniques of meditation is associated with the desire to be released from the isolated self. In the face of this it is not enough simply to affirm traditional Christian views. The usual pictures of heaven and hell are largely revolting to us. Even apart from our incredulity we are offended by their individualism. They deny our solidarity with one another in both good and evil.

Yet Christianity would no longer be Christianity if it abandoned its affirmation of the personal self. More than that, something that most of us prize very deeply would be lost to mankind. Christianity cannot make its contribution to the coming world faith by abandoning its greatest achievements. It must reconstitute these achievements in contemporary garb in order to go beyond them.

Hence we must think through more radically the meaning of love in relation to the personal self. I am suggesting that the isolation of the self is a function of lovelessness or imperfect love. I am suggesting that rather than abandon our selfhood we can perfect it in new kinds of communities of love. I am even suggesting that some of the methods for moving forward in this direction are already at hand.

Finally, we could only hope to move toward such a love if that love is grounded beyond ourselves. And it is. God loves us not only in that he actively seeks our good regardless of how we respond to him but in that he empathizes with us and takes our feelings into himself. We are in fact never alone. And because we are loved by God, we can also, in some small but perhaps growing measure, love each other. That is the meaning of Christ.

13

Joy

Joy is rare. Contentment, pleasure, gaiety, even happiness we can identify from time to time as we examine our moods and emotions. But joy goes beyond these. It is an experience that we associate with childhood. We remember from our early years, perhaps especially in connection with Christmas, whole hours of joy.

We should not sentimentalize childhood because it contains times of joy. It contains misery as well, a level of misery that we adults know only rarely. We are estranged from joy and saved from utter misery by the widening of our horizons and the growing complexity of our experience.

Childhood joy, like childhood misery, requires a complete immersion in the present. It allows for no side glances toward what others are feeling or thinking, no comparisons with earlier experiences or anticipations of future changes. Total involvement of the whole person is required. Such joy begins to fade about the time that Santa Claus becomes a pleasant fiction.

But we cannot be satisfied as adults with this loss of the possibility of childlike joy. We long for it, and we measure our happiness in relation to it. Our goal is its recovery in an adult form.

Christians have always been concerned to help people find joy. The history of Christianity is full of special methods and tech-

niques devised for this purpose. Monasticism, mystical disciplines, the Franciscan movement, and left-wing groups before
and after the Reformation offered ways of so simplifying and or-
dering experience that wholeness could be attained and adults
could know again something of the joy of the child.

Some Christian movements for the attainment of joy have
been intensely emotional. The sobersided Friends, whom we
think of as quiet and self-contained, once quaked for joy. That,
of course, is why they are still called Quakers. Likewise the
Shakers shook, and the Holy Rollers rolled. Today there is a
widespread recovery of joy through ecstatic speaking or speaking in tongues.

When such eighteenth-century revivalists as John Wesley,
George Whitefield, and Jonathan Edwards preached, they were
astonished by the intensity of feeling they aroused. Later revivalists aimed directly at arousing these feelings, culminating in
joy. Revivalism became a technique. Pietists, too, had their techniques for achieving and sustaining joy. The Oxford Group, and
the Moral Re-Armament movement which succeeded it, struc-
tured these techniques in one way. Camps Farthest Out struc-
tured them in another way.

But on the whole, revivalist and pietist techniques have played
out. The church now has little to offer in their place. Since
World War II the quest for joy has moved out of the churches
into the human potential movement. There new techniques have
been developed that work for many people. Alongside this Western development, and closely related to it, is the widespread interest in ancient techniques of the Orient, especially Yoga and
Zen.

What attitudes should we churchmen take toward this bur-
geoning quest for joy and the many responses which surround
us? First, we should regard it as a judgment upon us that those
who seek joy must look elsewhere. In our reaction against the
decadent pietism of the recent past, we falsely prided ourselves
on our willingness to accept life as it is, realistically, in all its

ambiguity, not painting it in more glowing colors. But we have found that people, indeed that we ourselves, remembering joy, will not settle for drabness.

We should be glad that, in a time when we have not known how to address this human longing, others have been able to help. We should be grateful, affirmative, and hopeful with regard to what they are doing. We should learn from them and critically appropriate for use in the church some of the techniques that have been developed outside the church.

Second, we should also retain a healthy skepticism. I hesitate to turn so quickly to this note, for it might seem to take back the word of praise and appreciation. I am sure that some of these techniques can produce joy, because I have experienced joy through them. I cherish the memory of those moments of joy. I am grateful to those who made them possible. I covet the same experience for others. We should not be skeptical about that.

But those who develop the techniques and those who received joy through them are likely to expect too much. Converts in Christian revivals often suppose that what has happened to them means that the joy they feel should pervade their lives. When it passes, they may feel more guilty and anxious than before, because they now believe that they have betrayed the spirit which saved them.

Richard Farson, together with Carl Rogers, was a leader of the Western Behavioral Science Institute for a number of years. He told me once that this problem is equally real for the human potential movement. He asserted that the subjective reports of those who spent time in the Institute's sensitivity and encounter groups were consistently glowing. I believed him, since I had written one of those glowing reports. But the results of a study of a research team hired by the Institute to determine effective change in the persons who had participated were negative. When people returned to the worlds from which they came, they returned also to the patterns of human relations from which they had been briefly liberated. I believed that, too, since that was my experience, although I do think that in subtle ways, hard for research teams to measure, the experience made a lasting difference.

Richard Farson's disappointment that the effects of human potential programs were temporary led him to leave that movement. He decided to work to change the environment of man rather than to concentrate on individual, inner change. But another response is now appearing.

We can see the importance of that response in the light of the eighteenth-century experience. Whitefield was a more effective preacher than Wesley. But Wesley organized his converts. Through class meetings, love feasts, and the singing of evangelical hymns, something of the joy experienced in conversion was retained and renewed. The results of Whitefield's revivals faded. Wesleyan churches still exist.

Instead of abandoning the human potential movement with Farson, other leaders are beginning to institutionalize it. One such leader is Werner Erhardt. Out of his wide experience with methods of facilitating human growth he has developed a program which he calls EST. This is a new synthesis of techniques from East and West. More impressive than his description of his program is the obvious joy of those who testify to what EST has meant to them. There is no doubt that they have experienced a quality of childlike wholeness which enables them to feel this new joy. But even more important than this testimony to what will inevitably prove to be a temporary intensity of joy is the institutional structure that seems to be emerging. There are ongoing support communities with regular meetings and rituals in which the rich experience of conversion can be renewed and strengthened. In EST or in some similar concept there may emerge out of the human potential movement a new "church."

However, even when the effects of conversion are institutionalized and thus made more lasting, they change us only in limited respects. Some techniques may free us to greater imaginative creativity; others, to more adequate expressions of love and caring; still others, to the greater enjoyment of our bodies. We may be enabled to break bad habits, to enter into community, or to assume responsibility. We may even learn to be open to God. But we find that no one of these new attainments, and no combination of them, is commensurate with our total being. We are strangely and wonderfully made. As persons we are infinitely complex. There are always more areas in which growth and change are needed. Each time we reach what we think is the top of the mountain, when the clouds of excitement lift, we see a ridge farther above us than we had previously supposed the pinnacle to be.

Furthermore, success brings new problems just because it is success. Moral and pious people, the saints and the sanctified, have a bad public image. They are now beginning to share this negative image with the psychoanalyzed, the liberated, and the sensitized. The negative image may be unfair, but it should serve as a warning. If I succeed in throwing off a bad habit by practicing a particular technique, if I share my knowledge with another, and if he still remains bound to the destructive habit, how do I feel? Do I not feel pleased with myself for what I have attained? Do I not feel that he who is still enslaved deserves his fate? Condescension, complacency, and self-righteousness lurk in the wings when any effective technique is used, threatening to poison the health that the technique brings.

Our Christian skepticism should not become an attack upon those movements which today offer the water of joy in a parched land. But it should enable us to say in a constructive way that more is required, that the effects pass quickly if new disciplines and structures of community do not sustain them, that life is very complex so that conversion must follow conversion, and that subtle checks are needed against the very present danger of the perversion of joy into self-righteousness.

The most important element in the appropriate Christian response to the quest for joy is a fresh consideration of the basis for Christian joy. Our tradition has always been interested in techniques for evoking joy. But more fundamentally Christianity has centered on its good news, its gospel. Christian joy is the response to that news.

That joy should come as a response to good news is nothing strange to us. All of us have experienced it. We have learned that the one we love loves us in return, that the job we wanted is offered to us, or that the child we thought lost has found his way. And in hearing that news, we have been flooded by joy.

The Christian good news is that God has entered the world for man's salvation, that he has made himself known in the helplessness of an infant and in a man dying on a cross. That news has implications. It means that we don't have to use techniques in order to be freed from everydayness. The world of everydayness is already livable when God's presence is recognized there.

But it is equally true that good news calls for a response, and part of that response is often the appropriate use of techniques which keep elements of the joy alive. For example, the news that the one we love loves us in return calls for actions which express and celebrate the mutual love and enhance and deepen it. We are free to learn ways and means of renewing the original joy evoked by the news. God is present in the techniques as well.

When we have heard the Christian good news, we experience the joy achieved by techniques in a new way. It is not an escape that we urgently need from an unendurable everydayness. It is instead an intensification and expansion of what is present everywhere, of what we can enjoy without the techniques as well. We can let the joy come and go without anxiety and without guilt. We don't have to be joyful, but we are free for joy.

Christianity is, therefore, not so much a technique for finding the joy of salvation as a message that, when it is really understood, evokes joy because it announces salvation. In this sense Christianity proclaims an objective reality rather than cultivating a subjective one, though it does not despise or oppose the cultivation of the subjective one as well.

That means also that the good news announced by Christianity is for all men. I as an individual am included. But if I hear the news rightly, I do not rejoice primarily because of what the news means privately for me. I rejoice because of what it means to everyone. If tomorrow we heard (what of course we will not hear) that real peace had come to Southeast Asia, that a new government had emerged representing all the people, that the United States was prepared to give billions through international channels to rebuild what our tens of billions have destroyed— if we heard all that, I would rejoice because of the relief from moral anguish I would feel privately and inwardly, and because of the renewed possibility of pride in being an American. But primarily we would rejoice together because of what the news would mean to all of us and even more to the noble and long-suffering people of Vietnam. Shared rejoicing about the good news for all people is more fundamental to the church than is private rejoicing over personal attainments.

It would be grossly unfair to suggest that those who find joy through techniques are insensitive to the needs of others. The pietist convert, like the participant in the human potential movement, is concerned that others too find joy. He may even take too much satisfaction in being an instrument of their salvation.

Yet we dare not be silent about the risk of the private search for joy that is likely to dominate the '70s. The man converted in pietist revivals and engrafted into the church was often changed in lasting ways. He became more disciplined, more responsible, gentler, a loyal member of the community, generous with his money, regular in prayer and Bible-reading, willing to engage in humanitarian service. But too often his prejudices against those of other cultures and races were not softened. Sometimes, even, he became less sensitive to wider social issues, believing that the same, very personal, means by which his own life had been soundly established should work for all, and ignoring the need for structural changes in society. The same dangers are inherent in the human potential movement.

The objectivity and universality of the good news should guard us as Christians against these dangers of privatism and individualism. It should establish a sense of our solidarity with all men in receiving the wholly unanticipated and undeserved gift. We are members of one another, and what God has done for us he has done for us all.

In vivid and characteristically exaggerated imagery Dostoevsky teaches us this Christian lesson in a story told in *The Brothers Karamazov*. (I am indebted for this story to Dorothee Sölle, who included it in her lecture, "The Role of Political Theology in Relation to the Liberation of Men," one of the plenary addresses at the conference on Religion and the Humanizing of Man, Sept. 1–5, 1972, Los Angeles.)

"Once upon a time there was a peasant woman and a very wicked woman she was. And she died and did not leave a single good deed behind. The devils caught her and plunged her into the lake of fire. So her guardian angel stood and wondered what good deed of hers he could remember to tell God. 'She once pulled up an onion in her garden,' said he, 'and gave it to a beggar woman.' And God answered: 'You take that onion then, hold it out to her in the lake, and let her take hold and be pulled out. And if you can pull her out of the lake, let her come to paradise, but if the onion breaks, then the woman must stay where she is.' The angel ran to the woman and held out the onion to her. 'Come,' said he, 'catch hold and I'll pull you out.' And he began cautiously pulling her out. He had just pulled her right out, when the other sinners in the lake, seeing how she was being drawn out, began catching hold of her so as to be pulled out with her. But she was a very wicked woman and she began kicking them. 'I'm to be pulled out, not you. It's my onion, not yours.' As soon as she said that, the onion broke. And the woman fell into the lake and she is burning there to this day. So the angel wept and went away."

The Christian news is objective and universal. In that way it counters our easy tendency toward subjectivity and individualism while also providing a context in which the quest for joy may be freely pursued.

The news is also important. It is that God has given himself to man for man's redemption, that is, that Christ, the Messiah, has come.

Cynthia Ozick, a Jewish writer, has noted the importance of this news. "For novelists it matters very much whether the Messiah has come or is yet to come. The human difference is this: If the Messiah has not yet appeared, then the world is still profane, and our task is to wrest him forth, to go and fetch him, so to speak—to do what is necessary to bring him on. But if the Messiah has already cleft the skin of human history, then the world is at this moment transfigured into a holy site, and we need only stand still; already redeemed, we do God's work unawares, and even the most unlikely vessels inherit the divine redemption." (Cynthia Ozick, *The New York Times Book Review,* June 11, 1972, p. 4. I am indebted for this quote to the editorial in *The Christian Advocate,* Dec. 21, 1972.)

The more important the news, the more is at stake in the finally decisive question. Is it true? The news comes to us bound up with legends, with an archaic world view, and with an anthropomorphic picture of God. Even when it is freed from these trappings, it seems to run counter to the continuing dominance of evil in human affairs.

But the Christian news can withstand these doubts. There *is* a power of life and growth, of healing and reconciliation, present to all humanity, indeed, in all things. In Jesus, God "has already cleft the skin of human history." And we as "the most unlikely vessels inherit the divine redemption." There is reason for joy.